TIGER TANK BATTALIONS
OF WORLD WAR II

SPEARHEAD

TIGER TANK BATTALIONS
OF WORLD WAR II

George Forty

ZENITH PRESS

PREVIOUS PAGE: Bitter weather on the Eastern Front. A platoon of Panzer-grenadiers pass a Tiger I during the winter of 1943/44. Freezing conditions like these played a significant part in the German defeat. *(BA 664/6758/33a)*

First published in 2008 by Zenith Press, an imprint of MBI Publishing Company, 400 First Avenue North, Suite 300, Minneapolis, MN 55401 USA

Copyright © 2008 by Compendium Publishing Ltd, 43 Firth Street, London W1D 4SA

Zenith Press titles are also available at discounts in bulk quantity for industrial or sales-promotional use. For details write to Special Sales Manager at MBI Publishing Company, 400 First Avenue North, Suite 300, Minneapolis, MN 55401 USA.

To find out more about our books, join us online at www.zenithpress.com.

ISBN-13: 978-0-7603-3049-4

Design: Compendium Design
Layout and editorial: Donald Sommerville
Maps: Mark Franklin

Printed in Singapore

CONTENTS

ORIGINS & HISTORY

> "The only instrument of armored warfare which German commanders regarded as qualitatively different from the rest was the Mark VI Tiger, which was not allotted to divisions but organized in independent battalions, kept under central control and committed to crucial offensive and counter-offensive missions."
>
> John Keegan, *The Second World War*

OPPOSITE: Tiger 131 was destined to become one of the best-known Tiger Is in the world, after being captured virtually undamaged, following an action with A Squadron, 48th Royal Tank Regiment, on April 21st, 1943. Subsequently it was brought to the U.K., inspected minutely then given to the Tank Museum, postwar, where it remained a star, but static, exhibit, until the end of the 20th century, when it was put back into full running order. Here it is seen with members of its original German crew. *(BA 787/510/10a)*

The Panzer Kampfwagen (PzKpfw) VI (Tiger) was probably the most famous tank of World War II, its fearsome reputation being out of all proportion to the actual numbers of Tigers to see action on any of the battlefields on the Eastern, Western or Mediterranean Fronts. Granted it did not have the same overall effect on the outcome of the war as did either the Soviet T-34 or the American M4 Sherman, yet the mere mention of its name struck fear into Allied tank crews, who knew that they would need all their skill, cunning—and a good deal of luck—to overcome such a worthy opponent, its combination of long-range firepower and solid protection more than making up for its considerable weight (56 tons) and below-average mechanical performance. To open this book on the German heavy tank units that were equipped with Tiger, it is relevant to start by looking briefly at the design and building of the tank and how it came into existence.

The first tank to be given the nomenclature "PzKpfw VI" was in fact the "new construction vehicle" (*Neubaufahrzeuge* or NbFz) of 1933–4; however, this was probably done only for propaganda reasons, development of the true "Tiger" not actually beginning until 1937, when Henschel und Sohn of Kassel was told to design and build a tank in the 30–33-ton range, to be known initially as DW1—the "breakthrough tank" (*Durchbruchswagen*). Its role was to be close infantry support and it would be armed with the same 7.5-cm howitzer as on the PzKpfw IV of the same era. A chassis was built and trials commenced, but they were halted in 1938, when the firm was told to switch its designers onto a much heavier, 65-ton, tank instead, known as VK 6501. However, after building two prototypes and starting trials,

Following the VK 3001 and VK 3601 projects came the heavier VK 4501. This is the Porsche entry into the design competition, also known as Tiger (P). Initially favored by Hitler, it never went into full production as the Henschel entry was clearly better. (*Author's Collection*)

the project was again stopped and Henschel told to go back to the DW1. By 1940 the company had produced an improved design, known as the DW2, weighing 32 tons, having a crew of five, a five-wheel torsion-bar suspension and being armed with the 7.5-cm L/24 howitzer, plus two machine guns, one of which was coaxial. Trials took place the following year but, before they could be completed, the Army Weapons Branch (*Heereswaffenamt*) altered the basic requirements, saying that the design had to be armed with the long-barrelled 7.5-cm L/48 gun. At the same time the Army brought three other firms into the project, inviting Porsche, MAN and Daimler-Benz all to tender as well as Henschel. The new tank was called the VK 3001 and it had a similar superstructure to the PzKpfw IV, but with a new suspension comprising seven interleaved bogie wheels and three return rollers. Henschel built four prototypes, known as the VK 3001(H), two in March 1941 and two in October 1941. However, by then the Soviet T-34/76 had made its dramatic first appearance on the battlefield, so it was decided to abandon this development in favor of the heavier VK 3601 (described below). The Porsche version, the VK 3001(P), also called the Leopard, had a number of new features including longitudinal torsion-bar suspension, while MAN and Daimler-Benz also produced their prototypes, but these and all the others were declared obsolete.

At the same time as work began on the VK 3001 design, the Heereswaffenamt placed an order for a 36-ton tank, the VK 3601—the specifications, it is said, coming directly from the Führer himself, including a top speed of 40 km/h (25 mph), thick armor and a high-velocity gun. Henschel built a prototype in March 1942, but even before it had appeared, work on both projects had virtually ceased in favor of yet another new tank, the VK 4501, which was designed to mount a version of the 8.8-cm FlaK 36 gun which Hitler certainly favored as it had already proved itself as an excellent anti-tank gun in ground combat. The Heereswaffenamt favored the use of a lighter gun (7.5-cm), so Krupp designed a heavier turret for the 8.8-cm weapon, while Rheinmetall designed the lighter one, but it never reached production.

In view of the limited time available Henschel decided to incorporate all the best features of the VK 3001(H) and VK 3601(H) designs into a new project—to be known as the VK 4501(H). There would be two models: H1 mounting the 8.8-cm gun, H2 the 7.5-cm gun. Porsche, which had also been told to compete, took much the same option, combining the best features of the VK 3001(P) design into the VK 4501(P)—also known as Tiger (P). After much hard work, both firms met the deadline and the trial took place at Rastenburg on the Führer's birthday, April 20th, 1942. The result was that H1 was clearly

Generaloberst Heinz Guderian, Inspector-General of Armored Forces, being shown over a Tiger I, belonging to 13./SS Panzer Regiment 1, during his visit in mid-April 1943. The tank (Turret No. 405) was the company commander's tank, so it was a Befehls-wagen fitted with extra radio sets that reduced the ammunition stowage from 92 to 66 rounds. *(BA 83/4/4)*

ABOVE & BELOW RIGHT: Front and rear three-quarter views of the U.K. Tank Museum's Tiger I maneuvering outside the museum. *(Tank Museum 71028-298 and 7024-033)*

the better of the two contestants, despite the fact the fact that a production order for 90 Tiger (P) was already in progress, with the first delivery scheduled for July 1942. (Tiger [P] was never produced as a tank, but most did see action as the Elefant tank destroyer, *see* Variants, page 91.) Nevertheless, common sense prevailed, H1 was chosen for production, to start in July/August 1942, with some 285 to be built by May 1943. At this point it is worth noting that each Tiger took some 300,000 man-hours to build at a cost of 800,000 Reichsmarks.

Thus began the production of the PzKpfw VI Ausführung H (Ausf H; *Ausführung* = Mark), which over the next three years would also be called: PzKpfw VI Tiger Ausf E, Tiger E, or Tiger I. First official British mention of the new heavy tank was contained in an AFV Technical Intelligence report, issued by MI 10 in February 1941; however, it was described as weighing 45 tons, with frontal armor 75 mm thick and mounting a 75-mm main gun, plus two further 2-cm guns and four machine guns. It was said to be 36 feet long, 10 feet wide and over 6 feet high, with a top speed of 25 mph and a crew of 18 (although it was commented that 13 was more appropriate)! Clearly German propaganda had been hard at work, as the comparative table shows:

	Tiger Ausf E	MI 10 guesstimate	NbFz
Length:	27 ft 8½ in	36 ft	24 ft
Width:	11 ft 8 in	10 ft	10 ft
Height:	9 ft 10 in	over 6 ft	8 ft 11 in
Weight:	56 tons	45 tons	24 tons
Armor (max):	100 mm	75 mm	70 mm
Crew:	5	13–18	6
Top speed:	23 mph	25 mph	22 mph

First Battlefield Actions

The first real evidence of the Tiger's existence appeared in the German press on December 11th, 1942, when a photograph was published in the *National Zeitung* showing a Tiger of the 501st Heavy Tank Battalion driving down a street in Tunis, North Africa. Actually Tiger had been blooded before then, its first two actions being unmitigated disasters. Thanks mainly to Hitler's impatience to get the type into action it was used hastily, in small numbers, and on unsuitable terrain. The first subunit with Tigers (four) was 1. Zug, schwere Panzer-Abteilung 502 (1st Platoon, 502nd Heavy Tank Battalion). This unit had left Fallingbostel by train with a small support echelon comprising elements of battalion HQ and the workshop company, including some technicians from Henschel, bound for Russia, arriving at Mga station (south-east of Leningrad) on August 29th, 1942. The tanks were then unloaded and moved up to the front line, arriving at their assembly point in thick forest at 1000 hours the following day. An hour later, the platoon mounted their tanks and started their engines. Leading the party was the 502nd Heavy Tank Battalion commander-to-be—Major Richard Märker—in his Tiger, accompanied by a Kübelwagen carrying Herr Franke from the Henschel factory. They married up with their infantry support, crossed the start line and began engaging targets. However, the ground was far too soft and unsuitable for such heavy tracked vehicles. Shortly after they had reached a low ridge the force divided, two Tigers going left and two right, but soon two broke down,

Production of Tiger I			
Month	1942	1943	1944
Jan	–	35	93
Feb	–	32	95
Mar	–	41	86
Apr	1	46	104
May	–	50	100
Jun	–	60	75
Jul	–	65	64
Aug	12	60	6*
Sep	15	85	–
Oct	15	50	–
Nov	17	60	–
Dec	23	65	–
Totals	83	649	623
Grand total			1,355

* Production ends

Production of the later Tiger II was only 377 in 1944 and a further 112 in 1945, giving a grand total of 489, far too few to keep the hard-pressed heavy tank battalions up to strength.

one with transmission problems and one with engine trouble. While Franke was arranging recovery, Märker arrived in his tank to say a third Tiger had also broken down, this time with steering problems. Recovery of all three was completed successfully during the night, despite the thick, heavy going, using three Sd Kfz 9 18-ton recovery tractors, to move each Tiger. All went well and fortunately the enemy did not appreciate what was happening. At the workshops the defective parts were rapidly stripped out and sent back by air to the manufacturers, who equally swiftly replaced them. They were then airlifted back again and the mechanics worked non-stop to fit them, so that by September 15th the tanks were again all ready for action.

Unfortunately, the second action was even less impressive. The four Tigers, plus some PzKpfw IIIs, were to spearhead an attack by the 170th Infantry Division on the Soviet Second Army on September 22nd. The area chosen for the attack was very similar to that of the abortive attack on August 29th. Vainly Major Märker protested, explaining that he had personally reconnoitered the ground and knew only too well how unsuitable it was for heavy tanks. However, the Führer himself would brook no argument! The attack began with a series of air strikes, then contact was made soon after crossing the start line and the leading Tiger

A column from II SS Panzerkorps *Das Reich* moving through woods in northern Russia, late in 1943. Note that there are both Tiger Is and PzKpfw IVs in the column, the Tigers being from the schwere SS Panzer-Kompanie *Das Reich*, which took part in rearguard actions around Zhitomir and Shepetovka in late 1943/early1944. *(BA 571/1721/26a)*

A captured Russian T-34 sits at the roadside under the shadow of a Tiger. The T-34 was an excellent medium tank, but no match for the Tiger in either firepower or protection. *(BA 457/65/36)*

was hit on the front glacis plate. It was not penetrated, but the explosion stopped the engine and it could not be restarted. The crew decided to abandon the tank and later someone threw a hand grenade into the turret and set it on fire. The other three Tigers all reached their first objective, but were then either knocked out or became stuck in the mud. Nevertheless, after much hard work, they were freed and all, except one, were recovered. During the night of September 24th a workshop party went forward, stripped the stranded tank as far as they could and crammed it full of ammunition so as to ensure as much destruction as possible, but of course it was no longer possible to keep the new tank a secret now that one was in enemy hands, albeit badly damaged. Poor Märker was the obvious scapegoat, and was swiftly posted to 5th Panzer Division and later killed in action. General Heinz Guderian, Inspector-General of Armored Troops (*Generalinspekteur der Panzertruppen*) and "father" of the *Blitzkrieg*, commented on the way that events had been handled in his *Memories of a Soldier*, published in 1960, in which he says:

> September 1942 also brought the first employment of the Tiger. An old lesson of war says that one must exercise patience in employing a new weapon until mass production, and therefore mass employment, is ensured. Hitler knew this. But he was itching to try out the big tank. He decided on a quite unimportant assignment, namely a local, limited counterattack on unsuitable terrain. The results were heavy losses, which could have been avoided, and the loss of secrecy and with it any future element of surprise. The disappointment was all the greater when the attack failed due to the unfavorable terrain.

For the next few months the Germans in that sector were forced onto the defensive, and, despite the unfavorable going, Tiger was able

It is August 1943 and this crew are making the most of being in a rest area on the southern shores of Lake Ladoga in northern Russia, to relax, have a swim, a general "make do and mend," and tidy up their Tiger I, before the next battle. *(BA 461/216/37a)*

to dominate the battlefield, thanks to its immensely accurate and powerful main armament, so that between January 12th and March 31st, 1943, the 502nd Heavy Tank Battalion, now complete, destroyed some 160 Soviet tanks for the loss of just six Tigers. On one occasion for example, the battalion received an urgent call from the 96th Infantry Division, saying that it was being overrun by two dozen Soviet T-34/76s. Four Tigers were sent to the rescue and, after knocking out half the enemy force, routed the remainder and forced them to retreat in confusion. Tiger had begun its battlefield conquests. The 8.8-cm armor-piercing shells had such a terrific impact that they would often rip off a T-34's turret, giving rise to the phrase: "The T-34 raises its hat whenever it meets a Tiger!"

Heavy Tank Battalions

Initially it had been proposed that every Panzer regiment would have its own Tiger company, but after a few months of operations it was clear that this would prove both impossible and impracticable. Such special weapon systems clearly needed to be carefully maintained—hence the need for a larger, more specialized workshop company with every heavy tank battalion—and their usage had to be tightly controlled. Therefore, it was decided to form special individual heavy tank battalions (schwere Panzer-Abteilung—s.Pz-Abt) that would operate on their own, though obviously in co-operation with other friendly forces. In other words they would be treated as army troops, available to be allocated, but only at the highest level. Hitler is said to have once remarked that each of these Tiger battalions was worth a complete Panzer division to him. Of course that is wildly exaggerating their actual battlefield influence, although tactically this was perhaps true in some local situations, while their immense propaganda effect undoubtedly cannot be discounted. Had it been possible to produce the tank in much larger numbers then its strategic influence on campaigns might well have been more pronounced. However, the 1,355 Tigers built at an average of just 54 a month could not be expected to work the miracles their Führer demanded of them.

Tiger Crewmen

Tiger crews were in the main all volunteers, generally in their late teens/early twenties, as the accompanying photographs show, although they were not, until much later in the war, brand new recruits, but rather experienced veterans from other units of the *Panzerwaffe*, either single volunteers or sometimes complete subunits. Thanks to the high level of protection offered by the Tiger the resulting low casualty rate among Tiger crewmen meant that this experience was retained and built upon within Tiger units. Training was handled in a modern way, a special Tiger training manual (*Tigerfibel*) being produced for basic mechanical training, which used cartoons, including "pin-ups," to get its messages across. This was in addition to two more serious handbooks for the driver and turret crew respectively, which were also produced by the department of the Generalinspekteur der Panzertruppen.

Additionally, there was also a primer that covered the tactical employment of the heavy tank battalions, explaining the various tactical formations that should be used at platoon and company level. Later on another pamphlet was produced, based upon the personal experience of Tiger commanders with first-hand battlefield knowledge, containing a number of most useful do's and don'ts for higher level commanders when employing Tigers. Unfortunately, like so many other wartime pamphlets produced by both sides, many of the relevant points these contained were disregarded, leading to the misuse of this all too precious commodity, the Tiger tank. Here, for example, are some of the more important points they tried to get across:

Reconnaissance and Re-supply Close liaison between Tiger commanders and the headquarters that is operationally responsible for them is vital from the outset, because everything involving Tigers—

Tiger Ancestors

The first German tank of the Nazi era was the PzKpfw I Ausf A. It was built from 1934 and served primarily as a light tank and for training. It weighed 5.4 tons and was armed with 2 x 7.92-mm MG 13 compared to the Tiger II, which weighed 68 tons and was armed with an 8.8cm KwK 43L/71 main gun and 2 x 7.92-mm MG 34.

such as, for example, reconnaissance, re-supply, etc.—takes much more time than with other tanks.

Orders Issue orders [for an attack or for movement] as early as possible to the Tiger commander(s) and, whenever possible, brief them first, because the Tigers will "carry the breakthrough" and need to be employed at the *Schwerpunkt* (focal point) of the attack.

Command Never put a Tiger unit under direct command of an infantry division in an attack, because the infantry lack troops who can keep pace with the Tigers, so they cannot exploit their successes nor can they hold the ground the Tigers have captured. Additionally, at the critical moment communications are bound to break down.

Movement Whenever possible Tiger units should move on their own, so as to keep the Tigers' engines running as smoothly as possible, thus reducing the wear and tear caused by continually stopping, starting, changing gear, etc. Also it will help to reduce the inevitable traffic jams at bottlenecks such as bridges.

Bridges Those classified as being only suitable for vehicles under 24 tons, will need reinforcing, but this can vary with weather conditions (heavy frost and ice will strengthen the bridge, continual rain will weaken it).

Engineers Send as many armored engineers as possible with the Tigers to deal with reinforcing bridges, improving fords, bridging anti-tank ditches, gapping minefields, etc.

Operations In order to ensure that the Tiger's potential is used to the best advantage careful pre-planning is vital before any operation. Listen to the Tiger commander—he is the expert!

Concentration of Force The Tiger unit must be the commander's main instrument of decisive action, so it should be concentrated at the focal point of the action.

Co-ordination Employ Tigers in co-ordination with other weapons, so that they can push through, reach and destroy enemy artillery, while others provide the necessary support (e.g. light tanks and assault guns to deal with heavy enemy infantry weapons, own artillery to suppress enemy artillery fire, tank-mounted Panzergrenadiers to capture and hold ground taken by the Tigers, finally, more light and medium tanks to exploit success).

An Allied Assessment

"Ordnance had dragged two disabled tanks to Monty's CP for his inspection. One was the squat 63-ton Tiger E Mark VI, the same kind that had outgunned our Shermans in the Tunisian djebels. Next to it stood a 50-ton Panther, Mark V. The Tiger carried a long-barreled 88 in its heavy round turret. On its breastplate the armor was seven inches thick. In Europe, as in Africa two years before, the Tiger could both out-gun and out-duel any Allied tank in the field. Fortunately for us, however, it was inadequately powered with a 650-hp engine and for that reason it frequently broke down. In fact losses from mechanical failure among these Tiger tanks probably exceeded those attributed to Allied guns in combat."

From: *A Soldier's Story*, General Omar N. Bradley

Workshop Locations Whenever possible provide workshops with suitable locations with solid foundations, where heavy cranes can be set up, as these are essential for their work. [The Tiger's turret had to be removed to replace the final drive unit and hence a massive portable gantry was an essential item for the maintenance company.] Additionally and ideally, these locations should be close to railway stations, so that they can deal with continual shipment of heavy spare parts.

Forced Marches Try to avoid forced marches as they put too much strain on the tanks' working parts (engine, transmission, running gear, etc.). The average hourly distance covered by a Tiger column should be 10 km by day and 7 km by night (6 or 4.5 miles); exceed these limits and you use up the Tiger's combat capability on the road rather than in action.

Travelling Try to have the Tigers move as little as possible, so as to reduce the wear on their heavy components.

Pauses Ensure that Tiger commanders are kept fully up to date as regards planned pauses in the fighting and do not order any standby

Summertime in Russia and denims or shirt-sleeve order appear to have been the order of the day for this crew from s.Pz-Abt 503. Note also the battlefield modification to their tank, with spare track plates held by a bar across the front of the hull. *(BA 85/105/15A)*

Factory fresh! A just completed Tiger I leaving the factory: 1,354 were built from August 1942 to August 1944. *(Tank Museum 2395/C5)*

alerts, so that Tiger crews can make the necessary arrangements for vital repair work to be completed during these pauses.

Repair and Recovery Do not assign Tigers to the field workshops and suchlike of other tank units, because they will lack the necessary specialist technicians, tools, and spare parts needed.

Stand-downs After a period of action Tiger units need some two–three weeks to work on their tanks to restore them to full fighting efficiency or their future performances will suffer.

In closing the pamphlet General Guderian said: "Where the Tiger unit was employed in concentration under the strict leadership of a skillful officer, it met with striking success. The main effect of the Tiger lay in the destruction of enemy tanks." (Quoted in Kleine & Kühn, *Tiger*)

READY FOR WAR

Formation

The very first Tiger units to be formed were 501. schwere Panzer-Kompanie and 502. s.Pz-Kp (501st and 502nd Heavy Tank Companies). These came into existence on February 16th, 1942. They were each to comprise nine Tigers 1s, together with ten PzKpfw III medium tanks.

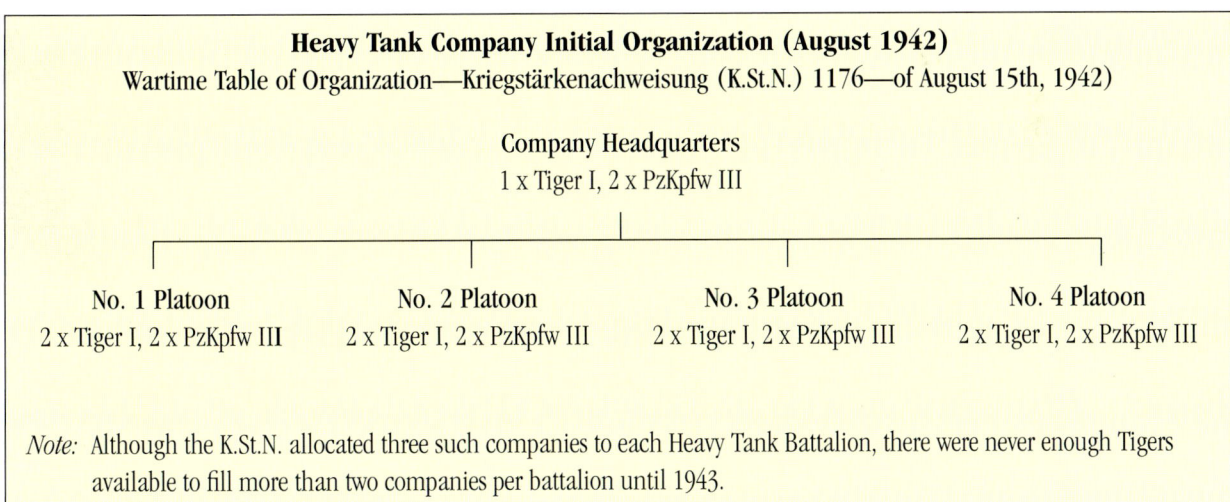

Heavy Tank Company Initial Organization (August 1942)
Wartime Table of Organization—Kriegstärkenachweisung (K.St.N.) 1176—of August 15th, 1942)

Company Headquarters
1 x Tiger I, 2 x PzKpfw III

No. 1 Platoon	No. 2 Platoon	No. 3 Platoon	No. 4 Platoon
2 x Tiger I, 2 x PzKpfw III	2 x Tiger I, 2 x PzKpfw III	2 x Tiger I, 2 x PzKpfw III	2 x Tiger I, 2 x PzKpfw III

Note: Although the K.St.N. allocated three such companies to each Heavy Tank Battalion, there were never enough Tigers available to fill more than two companies per battalion until 1943.

However, just over two months later (May 10th, 1942) the two companies were combined and became the cadre of the 501. schwere Panzer-Abteilung (s.Pz-Abt, Heavy Tank Battalion). Tank crews and other personnel for the first heavy tank units were recruited from existing tank battalions and Panzer und Ausbildung Abteilung 500 (Heavy Tank Replacement and Training Battalion 500) was formed at Paderborn. The 501st would not actually receive its Tigers until the autumn of 1942, after the second battalion formed (s.Pz-Abt 502) had already received some of its tanks and used them in action as already explained in Chapter 1. During the summer/fall these first two battalions would be joined by the 503rd, 504th, and 505th Heavy Tank Battalions. Each of these battalions had only two tank companies, still

An excellent comparison shot of the U.K. Tank Museum's Tiger I and PzKpfw III. *(Tank Museum 6395/F2)*

with just nine Tiger Is and ten PzKpfw IIIs, partly because of the lack of available Tiger tanks and partly because it was considered that the medium tanks could be used effectively against enemy infantry and anti-tank guns, thus providing close support for the Tigers. Indeed, the first official battalion organization additionally included a separate light platoon of ten PzKpfw IIIs that could be used for such tasks as flank protection. It also had an HQ company (Stabskompanie) and a workshop company (Werkstattkompanie) and when the battalions received more Tigers and changed their organization to three tank companies, they also reorganized and enlarged these other elements.

Further Expansion In addition to the five independent battalions, four infantry divisions were allocated heavy tank companies to be attached to their Panzer regiments, these were: Infantry Division *Grossdeutschland* (an Army unit) and three SS Divisions (1st *Leibstandarte SS Adolf Hitler* (*LSSAH*), 2nd *Das Reich* and 3rd *Totenkopf*. All four divisions were sent to southern Russia in early 1943, together with their heavy tank subunits. Meanwhile, the five initial heavy tank battalions had been sent to fight on the following battlefronts: 501st to Tunisia; 502nd to northern Russia; 503rd to southern Russia; 504th to Tunisia and Sicily; 505th to central Russia.

With the coming of spring 1943, and with more Tigers rolling off the assembly lines, a major expansion took place, each battalion being made up to the originally intended three heavy tank companies, with fourteen Tigers in each heavy company (two in HQ and three platoons each of four more). At battalion HQ, there were two Tiger command tanks (*Panzer Befehls Weg mit 8.8-cm KwK L/56*) plus one normal Tiger, so there were now 45 Tigers in each battalion. The necessary additional Tigers were sent out to those battalions already on operations, while those, such as the 501st and 504th, which had been virtually wiped out in action in North Africa and Sicily, would have to wait until they were re-formed before having their numbers made up.

Operational Usage Although some divisional and other senior commanders were inclined to split up heavy tank battalions and attach individual companies to formations, such a procedure was strongly advised against by General Guderian and his staff, not to mention the heavy tank battalion commanders themselves. A perfect example was in the allocation of 503. s.Pz-Abt within the southern pincer arm at Kursk, where individual companies were attached to individual Panzer divisions within III Panzer Corps for the opening moves. As can be imagined this placed enormous strain on the battalion's other companies (HQ, supply, and especially, workshops).

Additional Battalions Later in 1943, five more independent heavy tank battalions were formed and, after training, despatched to fight as follows: 506th to southern Russia; 507th to northern Russia; 508th to Italy; 509th to southern Russia; 510th to central Russia.

In addition, in 1943, the *Grossdeutschland* Division's heavy tank company was enlarged to full battalion size (it was the only heavy tank battalion to remain permanently attached to a division) and three more heavy tank battalions were formed by the Waffen-SS, initially being numbered 101st, 102nd, and 103rd (later to be renumbered 501st,

Every tank needs a hard-working, intelligent and capable crew to function properly on the battlefield and the Tiger was no exception. Although all five crew members had their own special jobs to do, they would work as a team on such tasks as ammunition replenishment, as seen here in the depths of winter on the Eastern Front. Crews would have to load some 92 of these long, heavy rounds, each weighing around 22 pounds, into the special internal ammunition racks. Note also the Zündapp motorcycle and sidecar. *(BA 277/847/31)*

502nd, and 503rd). Two would be sent to fight in France in June/July 1944 and be all but wiped out there, while the 103rd went to the Eastern Front. SS s.Pz-Abt 101 would gain a considerable reputation when part of its 2. Kompanie under the command of SS-Obersturmführer Michael Wittmann almost completely destroyed the entire advance guard of a British tank regiment at Villers-Bocage on June 13th, 1944.

Tiger II

Although not newly formed units, it is relevant here to mention those heavy tank companies/battalions that were later re-equipped with the even more powerful Tiger II. Initially there were only two such units: s.Pz-Abt 503 and a schwere Funklenk-Kompanie (demolition carriers) attached to the Panzer Lehr Division, both being the first to be equipped with the new tank and to use it in battle. Of the other heavy tank battalions, the following were partly or completely re-equipped with Tiger II (also known as the King Tiger).

Served only on the Eastern Front: 501, 505, 507, 509, SS 503
Served only in the West: 506
Served in both the West and Hungary: 503, SS 501, SS 502

Gun cleaning was another vitally important task, needing at least two of the crew. Note the double-baffle muzzle brake on the end of the barrel. The gun was electrically fired and used similar ammunition to the 8.8-cm FlaK 18, but had different recoil gear so as to enable it to be fitted into a tank. *(BA 455/20/23)*

Renaming Other Heavy Tank Battalions As already mentioned, the three SS Heavy Tank Battalions (101st, 102nd, and 103rd) were later renamed the 501st, 502nd, and 503rd. However, so as not to confuse them with the three similarly named Army battalions, these latter Army units were renamed as shown in the table.

Name Changes		
Old	*New*	*Date changed*
501st	424th	21 Dec 44
502nd	511th	9 Jan 45
503rd	*Feldherrnhalle*	
		21 Dec 44

Demolition carriers

Two other specialized units would be given a complement of Tiger tanks (initially Tiger I and later Tiger II). These were:

Panzer-Abteilung (Funklenk) 301 A specialized battalion containing a mixture of Tiger I tanks and Ladungsträger (demolition carriers) was established in Russia in early September 1942 by the redesignation of Panzer-Abteilung (Funklenk) 300. However, it was not until October 1944 that the unit began to receive Tiger tanks with which to control its demolition carriers remotely.

Panzer-Kompanie (Funklenk) 316 This specialized company was initially established as an armored experimental and replacement unit in the spring of 1943, but that summer was redesignated as above and later re-equipped with a mixture of both Tiger I and Tiger II, plus of course the demolition carriers

Organization

For the initial campaigns of the war the PzKpfw IV tank in the normal tank regiment/division had taken the place of the true heavy tank that was non-existent in the *Panzerwaffe* until the arrival of Tiger, and later Panther. PzKpfw IV had performed perfectly well against everything the Allies could field against it, until such AFVs as the Russian KV-1 and -2 heavy tanks had to be faced, and, most importantly, the T-34/76 medium tank. The T-34's remarkable sloped armor and all-round excellence had made the Germans realize they were in danger of falling well behind in the tank-versus-tank battle if they could not get their heavy Tiger that was still waiting in the wings into service. The need for a tank with a larger, more powerful anti-armor gun and thicker armor to protect its crew and weapon system—in other words Tiger—was now clear for all to see. However, it was also soon clear that this solution to

Maintenance/repair to the tank's suspension was always hard work—not made any easier sometimes by the state of the ground and bad weather conditions. The mechanics would naturally help crews with the work which, as can be seen, was both difficult and dirty, especially where repairs involved the interleaved roadwheels and torsion bars. In January 1944, new steel-tired rubber-cushioned roadwheels replaced the dished type. Photograph taken in Italy, February 1944. *(BA 310/898/25)*

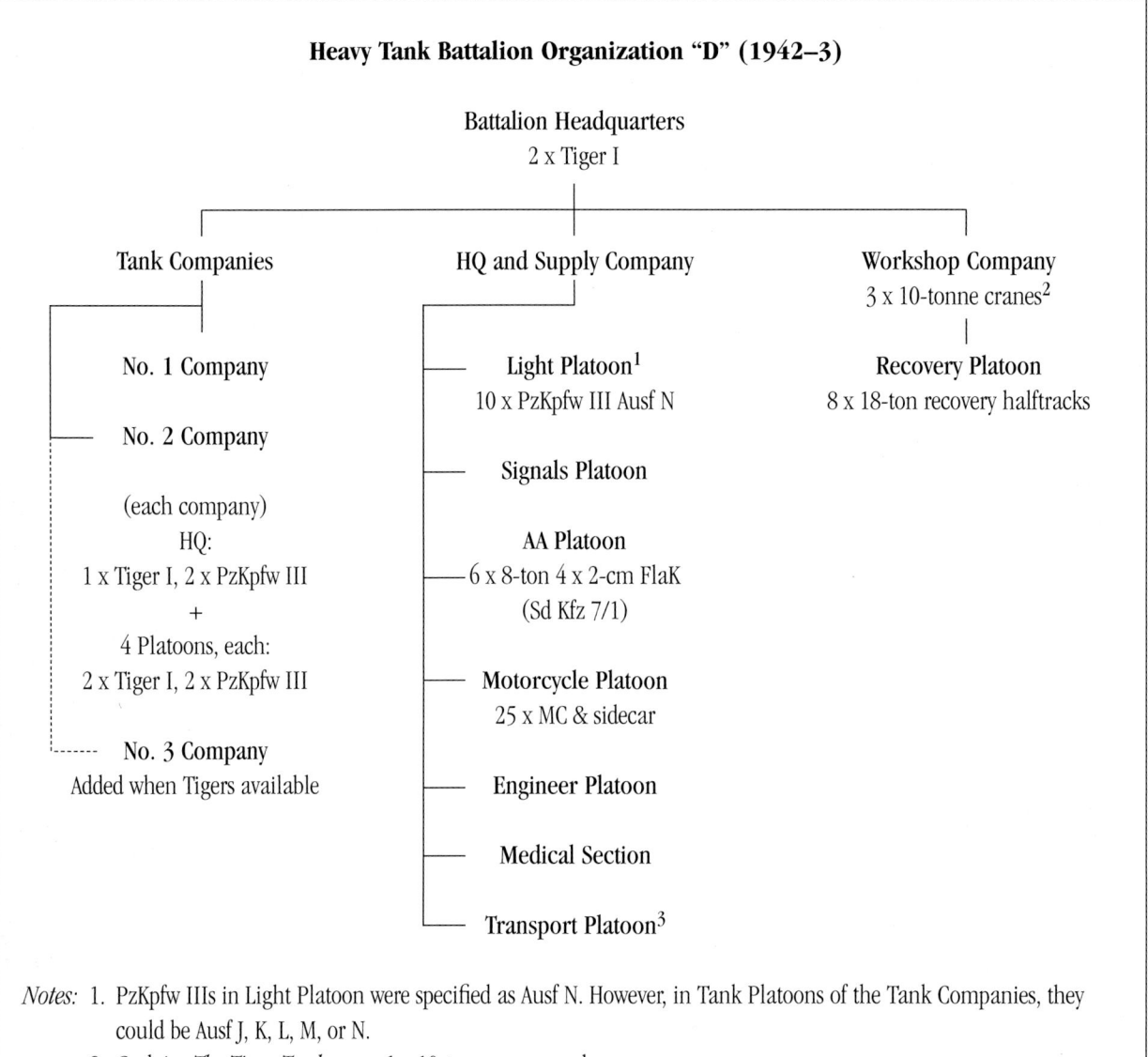

Heavy Tank Battalion Organization "D" (1942–3)

Battalion Headquarters
2 x Tiger I

Tank Companies

No. 1 Company

No. 2 Company

(each company)
HQ:
1 x Tiger I, 2 x PzKpfw III
+
4 Platoons, each:
2 x Tiger I, 2 x PzKpfw III

No. 3 Company
Added when Tigers available

HQ and Supply Company

Light Platoon[1]
10 x PzKpfw III Ausf N

Signals Platoon

AA Platoon
6 x 8-ton 4 x 2-cm FlaK
(Sd Kfz 7/1)

Motorcycle Platoon
25 x MC & sidecar

Engineer Platoon

Medical Section

Transport Platoon[3]

Workshop Company
3 x 10-tonne cranes[2]

Recovery Platoon
8 x 18-ton recovery halftracks

Notes: 1. PzKpfw IIIs in Light Platoon were specified as Ausf N. However, in Tank Platoons of the Tank Companies, they could be Ausf J, K, L, M, or N.

2. Gudgin, *The Tiger Tanks*, says 1 x 10-tonne crane only.

3. See table on page 96 for details of the types of vehicles.

Germany's problems could not be produced quickly enough, and in sufficient quantity, to fill the bill immediately and that the *Panzerwaffe* would, at least for the time being, have to make do with a compromise solution. This compromise was to form battalions with just two tank companies, each of four platoons, each of two Tiger Is and two PzKpfw IIIs (model unspecified). Additionally there would be a further Tiger at company HQ (for the commander) and two at battalion HQ, making a total of 20 Tigers and 16 PzKpfw IIIs in the battalion.

Although this was primarily due to the shortage of Tigers as production could not be speeded up overnight, it did not help, for example, that eight of the Tigers belonging to the very first heavy tank battalion to be sent overseas (501st to Tunisia) were diverted to southern France on the direct order of the Armed Forces High Command (Oberkommando der Wehrmacht—OKW) to guard against any problems with the occupation of that part of Vichy France. Thus the battalion that was shipped to Tunisia consisted of just one company of four tank platoons of two Tigers and two PzKpfw IIIs each, with two Tigers at company HQ and two more at battalion HQ, plus supporting supply and repair elements. The Tigers were intended to be the PzKpfw VI (P) built by the Porsche factory, which had air-cooled engines and were thus considered more suitable for operating in the heat of North Africa. However, drive-train problems slowed their production and the five completed Tiger (P) were eventually issued for training at Döllersheim. The remaining eight PzKpfw IIIs which lacked their matching Tigers were concentrated together into a light platoon so the battalion's total tank numbers were twelve Tigers and sixteen PzKpfw IIIs. Finally, the eight missing Tigers, still in France, were organized into two platoons of four each.

A mechanic at work on the Maybach HL210 (or 230 on later models) V-12 water-cooled gasoline engine that powered Tiger I and was mounted centrally to the rear of the tank. (BA 278/874/32)

That was, of course, just the tank element of the battalion, in addition there was a workshop company (which included a recovery platoon) and a headquarters company. This organization was known by the letter "D" and was the standard heavy tank battalion organization for 1942–3.

Internal Company Organization Within companies, the standard tank platoon of two Tigers and two PzKpfw IIIs was, as the diagram shows, the norm for heavy tank battalions of that period. However, battalion commanders naturally tried a variety of internal organizations to discover which one was the most suitable for a particular operation or

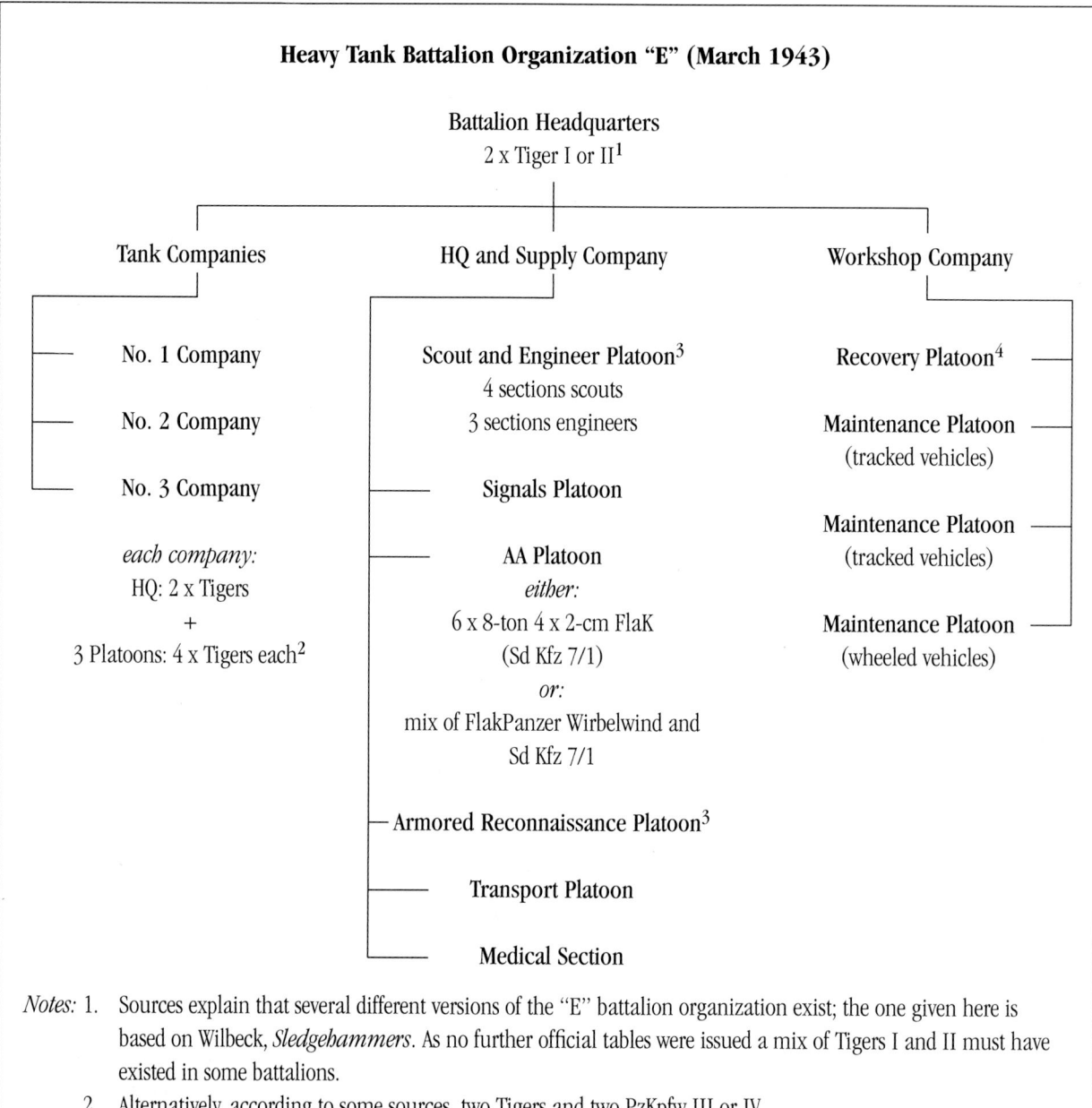

Heavy Tank Battalion Organization "E" (March 1943)

Battalion Headquarters
2 x Tiger I or II[1]

Tank Companies

HQ and Supply Company

Workshop Company

No. 1 Company

No. 2 Company

No. 3 Company

each company:
HQ: 2 x Tigers
+
3 Platoons: 4 x Tigers each[2]

Scout and Engineer Platoon[3]
4 sections scouts
3 sections engineers

Signals Platoon

AA Platoon
either:
6 x 8-ton 4 x 2-cm FlaK
(Sd Kfz 7/1)
or:
mix of FlakPanzer Wirbelwind and
Sd Kfz 7/1

Armored Reconnaissance Platoon[3]

Transport Platoon

Medical Section

Recovery Platoon[4]

Maintenance Platoon
(tracked vehicles)

Maintenance Platoon
(tracked vehicles)

Maintenance Platoon
(wheeled vehicles)

Notes:
1. Sources explain that several different versions of the "E" battalion organization exist; the one given here is based on Wilbeck, *Sledgehammers*. As no further official tables were issued a mix of Tigers I and II must have existed in some battalions.
2. Alternatively, according to some sources, two Tigers and two PzKpfw III or IV.
3. The "E" organization has lost the Light Tank Platoon but gained an Armored Recce Platoon as well as enlarging the Engineer Platoon to include a scout element. This platoon could classify and reinforce bridges, clear mines and other obstacles.
4. From the end of 1944 Recovery Platoons contained a mix of up to five Bergepanther V and up to seven Sd Kfz 9 18-ton recovery vehicles.

situation. For example, some formed separate medium and heavy companies, with all the PzKpfw IIIs in the medium company and all the Tigers in the other, or varied the mix within companies to suit the particular circumstances.

Enlargement

When the battalion changed to incorporate a third tank company there was also a need to enlarge the maintenance and supply elements, so a separate supply company (*Versorgungskompanie*) was formed in addition to HQ company, and the workshop company was enlarged to include two platoons for tracked vehicle repairs and a third platoon for wheeled vehicles; in addition, of course, there was still a separate recovery platoon (*Bergezug*). Tank companies now had an HQ section, a medical section, a maintenance section and their own small supply train.

Total tank company strength was 113 men, manning 14 tanks and 22 wheeled vehicles, while the battalion total strength was 1,093 all ranks made up of: 28 officers, 274 NCOs, and 694 enlisted men; the remaining 97 were seven civilian maintenance personnel and 90 "Hiwis" (abbreviation for *Hilfswillige* who were Russian soldiers, either captured or deserters, who had agreed to serve in the German armed forces).

Toward the end of the war the battalion manpower was reduced to 895 plus seven civilians, organized as shown in the table.

The new enlarged organization was known as the "E" organization and, although approved in March 1943, took some time to become effective within all heavy tank battalions.

Waffen-SS

In April 1943, orders were published concerning the establishment of a new Tiger battalion for the I SS Panzerkorps. Although a new HQ staff was organized, the unit's three companies, raised some months earlier during November 1942 and allocated to the three SS Divisions (*LSSAH*, *Das Reich*, and *Totenkopf*), remained with their SS Divisions and were also materially strengthened by the replacement of their PzKpfw IIIs with Tiger Is. In June 1943, I SS Panzerkorps became II SS Panzerkorps with the raising of the new I SS Panzerkorps *Adolf Hitler*, which then had its own new

Late War Battalion Manpower
Tank Companies (each)
4 officers, 46 NCOs, 38 enlisted men (company train personnel now part of the supply company)
Supply Company
5 officers, 55 NCOs, 188 enlisted men
Headquarters Company
9 officers, 37 NCOs, 130 enlisted men
Maintenance Company
3 officers, 37 NCOs, 167 enlisted men
Source: Schneider, *Tigers in Combat*

Seldom did tank crews get a chance to have hot food and the time to eat it. Here a full Tiger crew of five tuck in to a meal out of their mess tins, while sitting on their tank *(BA 277/846/8)*

The workshop company needed space and hard standing to set up its portable 10-tonne gantry crane, with which they could lift the turret of a Tiger I—as seen here. *(BA 278/875/31A)*

"all Tiger" battalion. The Tiger company that had been with the *LSSAH* Division was re-assigned to the new I SS Panzerkorps heavy tank battalion as its third company, a new company being raised in the II SS Panzerkorps battalion to replace it. These became the 1st and 2nd SS Heavy Tank Battalions. On October 22nd, 1943, the names of the SS heavy tank battalions were altered by adding 100 to their titles so that they became the 101st and 102nd. They would be joined by the 103rd, which was sent to fight in Russia rather than in the west as was the case with the other two. In line with other Waffen-SS units, the SS heavy tank battalions received a full complement of tanks, weapons and equipment, so that when they were sent to fight they were up to full establishment.

IN ACTION

OPPOSITE: The Tunisian campaign. The operational areas for Heavy Tank Battalions 501 and 504 are shown.

Tunisia

Schwere Panzer-Abteilung 501 was established on May 10th, 1942, at Erfurt, capital of Thuringia in central Germany, under the command of Major Hans-Georg Lueder, by combining the two independent Heavy Tank Companies 501 and 502, together with additional personnel from both the local 1. Panzer-Ersatz-Abteilung (Armored Replacement Battalion 1), and the neighboring tank gunnery school at Putlos (see table for details of locations and dates where and when all the battalions were first formed). A few days later the new unit moved to the Ohrdruf Training Area to begin its Tiger training. In late August, it received its first Tiger Is and by October it had 20 Tiger Is and 16 PzKpfw IIIs of various Marks, organized on a two-company basis, with four platoons of two Tigers and two PzKpfw IIIs per platoon. They were soon warned for service in Tunisia, where on November 8th, 1942, the Allies would

Locations Where Formed		
Heavy Tank Battalion	*Location*	*Date*
501st (later 424th)	Erfurt	May 1942
502nd (later 511th)	Bamberg	May 1942
503rd (later *Feldherrnhalle*)	Neuruppin	April 1942
504th	Fallingbostel	January 1943
505th	Fallingbostel	January 1943
506th	St Pölten	July 1943
507th	Vienna/Mödling	September 1943
508th	Heilbronn	July/August 1943
509th	Schwetzingen	September 1943
510th	Paderborn	June 1944
III./GD	Sennelager	June 1943
301st (Funklenk)	Grafenwöhr	October 1944
SS 101st (later 501st)	Sennelager	July 1943
SS 102nd (later 502nd)	Sennelager	July 1943
SS 103rd (later 503rd)	Paderborn	spring 1944

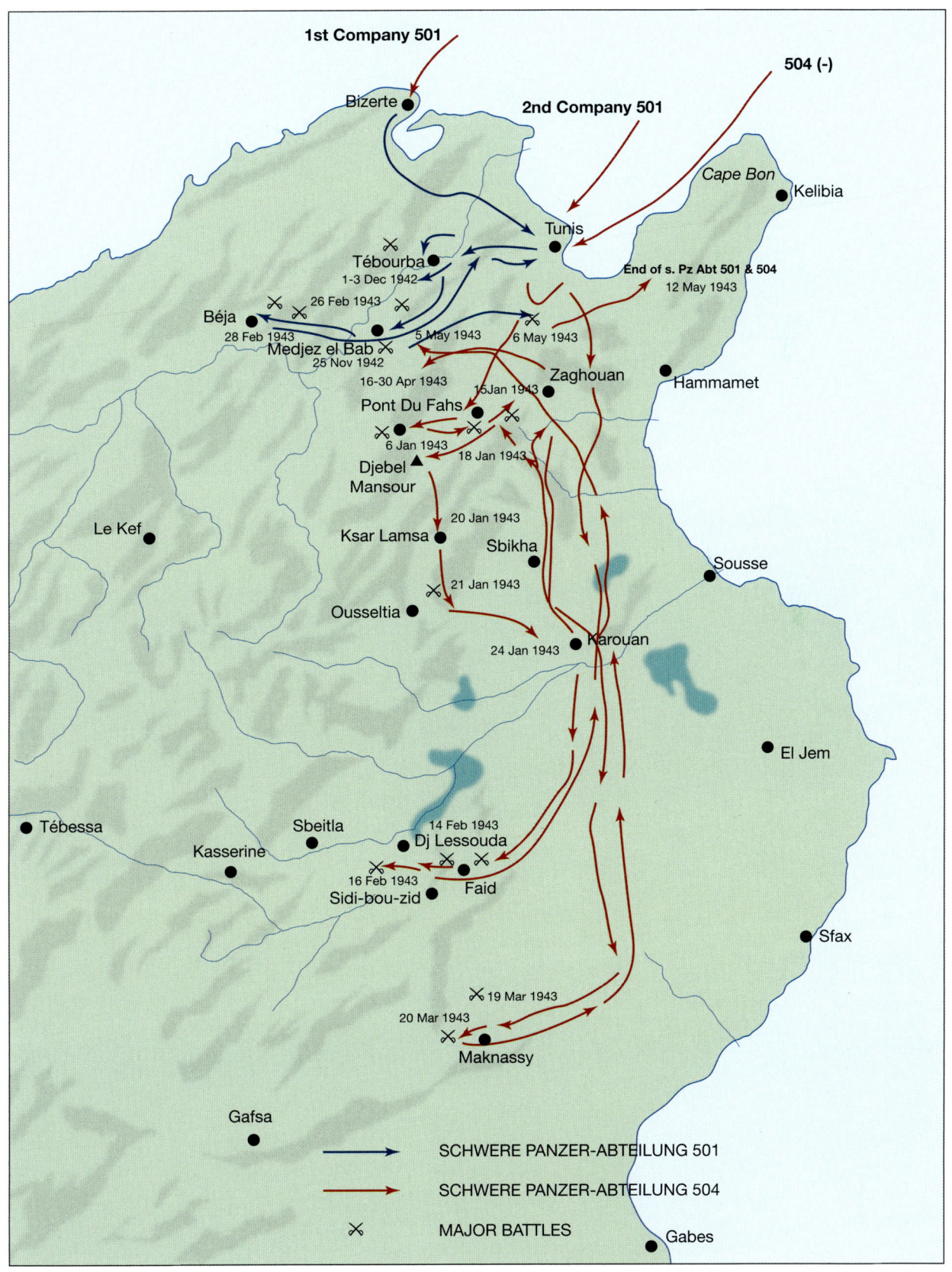

1st Company 501

2nd Company 501

504 (-)

Bizerte

Cape Bon

Kelibia

Tunis

End of s. Pz Abt 501 & 504
12 May 1943

Tébourba
1-3 Dec 1942

26 Feb 1943

Béja
28 Feb 1943

Medjez el Bab
25 Nov 1942

5 May 1943

6 May 1943

Zaghouan

Hammamet

16-30 Apr 1943

Pont Du Fahs

15 Jan 1943

6 Jan 1943

18 Jan 1943

Djebel
Mansour

20 Jan 1943

Ksar Lamsa

Sbikha

Le Kef

Sousse

21 Jan 1943

Ousseltia

24 Jan 1943

Karouan

El Jem

Tébessa

Sbeitla

14 Feb 1943

Dj Lessouda

Kasserine

16 Feb 1943

Faid

Sidi-bou-zid

Sfax

19 Mar 1943

20 Mar 1943

Maknassy

Gafsa

Gabes

SCHWERE PANZER-ABTEILUNG 501

SCHWERE PANZER-ABTEILUNG 504

MAJOR BATTLES

Meet the locals. The Tunisians did not seem to like or dislike either the Allied or Axis forces, or to favor one side over the other. However, they certainly took an interest in the German weaponry on its arrival, especially the massive Tiger tanks of 501st Heavy Tank Battalion, the first Tigers to arrive in Tunisia in November 1942. *(BA 420/2033/20A)*

invade from the sea (Operation Torch), roughly in step with General Montgomery's British and Commonwealth forces' advance from El Alamein.

Movement by rail followed for the heavy tank battalion, through southern France and Italy, to the Italian port of Reggio/Calabria on the Straits of Messina. However, not all the battalion moved there, the 2nd Company being diverted to the south of France on orders from OKW for internal security duties. The following month the battalion's tanks (less the 2nd Company) were embarked for Bizerte in Tunisia, while the crews were transported by air, including Major Lueder, who went ahead of the main body. On September 16th, 1942, British codebreakers were able to decrypt a message from German Army headquarters advising Rommel's Panzerarmee Afrika HQ of the Tiger I's vital statistics, a

useful indication that a Tiger unit was soon to be on its way to North Africa. Some weeks later there was another message querying when the expected tanks would arrive; the answer (also decrypted) advised that the first batch would be arriving in November and a further consignment the following month.

Meanwhile, it had been decided that Major Lueder would initially command a combat team (*Kampfgruppe*) to support Airborne Task Force *Koch* in the area near Medjez-el-Bab, the battalion's tanks joining him as and when they arrived. They were soon hard at work being trained in desert warfare by an experienced Deutsches Afrika Korps officer. A few days later, after the Allied Torch landings had taken place, they were involved in heavy fighting around the Tébourba–Medjez-el-Bab area, their first battle being at Medjez-el-Bab station on November 25th. They eventually took Tébourba on December 4th, knocking out numerous American tanks and, most importantly, preventing them from breaking out to the west. After the battle the combat team was disbanded and Lueder and his battalion were then transferred to Manouba near Tunis. They continued to operate despite losses, mainly through breakdowns, replacements arriving in early December 1942, having been transported by rail from Fallingbostel to Trapani, a port on the west coast of Sicily, then ferried across to Tunisia. By December 25th the 501st had increased in strength to twelve Tigers and sixteen PzKpfw IIIs. At the beginning of January 1943, 2nd Company started to arrive and by the middle of the month both Tiger companies were up to full strength for the first time.

Throughout this period the company continued to operate as a local "fire brigade," easily dealing with most of the Allied opposition whose

> **German Tank Production**
> Nazi Germany built approximately 6,109 tanks starting in 1934 through 1939, then a further 24,350 in 1940–45, a total of 30,459 (compared with 88,410 built in the U.S.A. during 1940–45.

6-pounder and 75-mm guns (on such tanks as the British Crusader and Valentine and the American M3 and M4) were outclassed by the Tiger's 8.8-cm main armament and its thick armor. Even Tiger's side armor was impervious to the Allied armor-piercing ammunition at ranges over 650 yards.

Later the battalion would take part in a major German attack, Operation Eilboete, which began on January 18th. General von Arnim's plan was to capture all five of the passes through the Eastern Dorsales range, in order to give Axis forces a series of launching pads from which they could strike into the Tunisian plain beyond. The Tigers of the 501st played their part as members of a battle group deployed in the area south-west of Pont-du-Fahs and Zaghouan. They were hampered considerably by well placed Allied minefields, covered by a screen of 6-pounder anti-tank guns, and also by the serious lack of replacement Tiger roadwheels and other spares. During the action, anti-tank guns belonging to 72nd Anti-Tank Regiment, Royal Artillery, knocked out two Tigers, proving that they were not invulnerable. The Allies managed to hold on to the vital Kasserine Pass and the Axis attack ran out of steam. This action would be followed later by two more major operations: Frühlingswind and Ochsenkopf and many minor ones. The first of the two resulted in nearly seventy U.S. tanks being destroyed, of which many were knocked out by 1st Company of the 501st. A few

In February 1943, both companies of s.Pz-Abt 501 became part of Kampf-gruppe *Lang* and the battalion was incorporated into Panzer Regiment 7 of 10th Panzer Division, as its 3rd battalion. Thus, 1st Company, 501st, became 7th Company, Panzer Regiment 7, hence the turret renumbering, as here, to "732." *(BA 562/1164/26A)*

This Tiger (142) was the second tank of 4th Platoon, 1st Company, 501st, so had been one of the first to arrive in Tunisia. It is seen here later (in 1943) during one of the major Axis operations against the Allies. *(BA 788/17/3)*

days later, the company was ordered to deal with a concentration of U.S. armor north-west of Sidi-bou-Zid. It did so, again knocking out a large number of American tanks and wheeled vehicles. Operation Ochsenkopf's aim had been to capture Medjez-el-Bab. However, not only did it not succeed, it also led to numerous unwelcome Tiger casualties from a well-laid British anti-tank gun ambush at a defile known as Hunt's Gap.

Arrival of the 504th Despite being very short of spares, the Tigers of the 501st fought on until the final German surrender on the Bône Peninsula in May 1943. However, before this took place, they had been joined in North Africa by part of another heavy tank battalion, s.Pz-Abt 504. This battalion had been formed at Fallingbostel on January 18th, 1943, and Major August Seidensticker appointed as CO shortly after. The battalion was then transported by rail to Italy and thence to Sicily in early March 1943. The leading company was shipped over to Tunis together with elements of the HQ and workshop companies. Their arrival would provide the remaining Tigers that Hitler had promised Rommel. However, the 2nd company of the 504th stayed in Sicily and would not see action until the Allied landing there in mid-July 1943. On the arrival of the 504th's main body in Tunis in early March 1943, the unit absorbed the remaining 11 Tigers of the 501st, which was at the time without a battalion commander. The combined unit, comprising what was left of the 501st and the 504th (still minus the one company in Sicily) then moved from Tunis via a difficult 250-mile road march to the Sfax– Maknassy area, arriving on March 19th. Here, at the Maknassy Pass, under the command of Major Seidensticker, and despite heavy Allied bombing and a massive artillery barrage, they stopped a force comprising the U.S. 1st Armored Division and the U.S. 9th Infantry Division plus an additional brigade group, knocking out some 44 tanks.

The 501st/504th would continue to be involved in heavy fighting right up to the end in North Africa, when the remaining tanks of both battalions would have to be destroyed by their crews. During the fighting in Tunisia, however, one of the 504th Battalion Tigers (Turret No. 131) was captured virtually undamaged and shipped to the U.K. During the two months it had operated in Tunisia, the 501st had accounted for over 150 Allied tanks, while the 504th had also destroyed roughly the same number—a remarkable success rate, bearing in mind that there were, by comparison with other AFVs, just a mere handful of Tigers present in Tunisia at any one time and never more than about twenty serviceable. Even when one accepts the fact that all the Tigers taken to North Africa were eventually lost when the Axis forces surrendered on May 12th, 1943, it is a remarkable record and enough to lay the foundations of the myth of Tiger invincibility.

Sicily

Despite the surrender in Tunisia, the 501st would live again, being re-constituted in Paderborn on September 9th, 1943, its nucleus being some 150 ex-members of the original 501st, who had been withdrawn from Tunisia before the surrender, minus their tanks. Later, in early December 1943, after training at the Mailly-le-Camp Training Area near Reims in France, the re-formed 501st would be sent to Russia. As already mentioned, only one company of the 504th had been shipped over to Tunisia, the other company remaining in Sicily, where it would be made up to a strength of seventeen Tigers (it handed over its non-Tiger tanks to Pz-Abt 215) by mid-June 1943. When Operation Husky (the Allied invasion of Sicily) began on July 10th, several of the Tigers engaged the incoming landing craft until they were themselves engaged by naval gunfire and had to withdraw. Thereafter the Tigers were, as usual, heavily involved in the fighting. For example in the area of

The Origins of Blitzkrieg

"The expression 'Blitzkrieg' is an Italian invention. We picked it up from the newspapers. I've just learned that I owe all my successes to an attentive study of Italian military theories."

From: *Hitler's Table Talk 1941–44, His Private Conversations*, ed. H. R. Trevor-Roper (January 3rd/4th 1942)

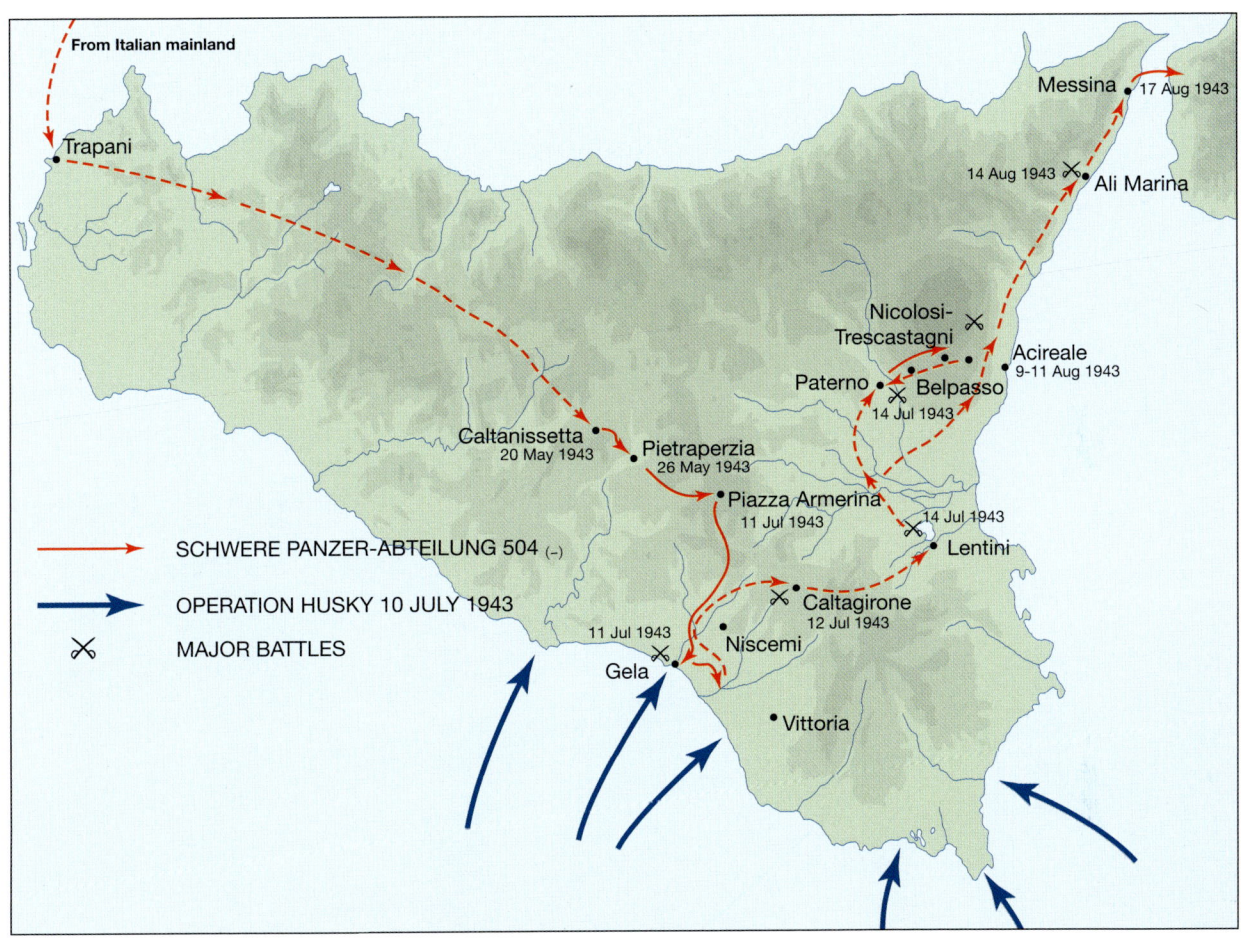

From Italian mainland

Trapani

Messina • 17 Aug 1943

14 Aug 1943 ✕ Ali Marina

Nicolosi-
Trescastagni ✕

Acireale
9–11 Aug 1943

Paterno ✕ Belpasso
14 Jul 1943

Caltanissetta
20 May 1943

Pietraperzia
26 May 1943

Piazza Armerina
11 Jul 1943

14 Jul 1943
✕ Lentini

Caltagirone
12 Jul 1943

11 Jul 1943
✕
Niscemi

Gela

Vittoria

→ SCHWERE PANZER-ABTEILUNG 504 (–)

→ OPERATION HUSKY 10 JULY 1943

✕ MAJOR BATTLES

Vittoria in southern Sicily, a group of five Tigers was surrounded, but knocked out sixteen Allied tanks for the loss of three Tigers destroyed. The remaining two withdrew, but eventually had to be blown up after running out of fuel. By mid-August the company was down to just one fit Tiger, the others having been knocked out or having broken down and been destroyed by their crews. This last Tiger was transported by a Siebel ferry across the Straits of Messina. However, it broke down soon after arrival, could not be repaired, and so had to be destroyed. With the capture of Messina on August 17th all resistance in Sicily ended and, with it, there came a temporary end for the 504th, which would not be reconstituted until the end of 1943, when it would return to northern Italy.

The operations in Sicily in July–August 1943 by part of s.Pz-Abt 504.

Italy

The Allied campaign in mainland Italy began on September 3rd, 1943, when the British Eighth Army crossed the Straits of Messina (Operation Baytown), to be followed on September 9th by the U.S. Fifth Army landings at Salerno (Operation Avalanche). British airborne troops also landed that day in the Gulf of Taranto as the British advanced through

ABOVE : A photograph taken in the Nettuno area near Anzio. This crew has its problems with a broken track. At least they are covered from aerial view by the trees. *(BA 311/904/29)*

LEFT: In the Aprilia sector, just north of Anzio, during the second half of February 1944. The 508th Battalion tanks had some 50 percent mechanical breakdowns during the journey. *(BA 310/880/26a)*

BELOW: A Sturmpanzer IV (Brummbär), passing a broken-down Tiger in the Nettuno area, March 1944. Luckily, a recovery half-track (an 18-ton Zugkraftwagen) was in the vicinity and was about to come to the rescue. *(BA 311/903/23)*

Anzio: s.Pz-Abt 508's attack on the Allied beachhead on February 16th–18th, 1944.

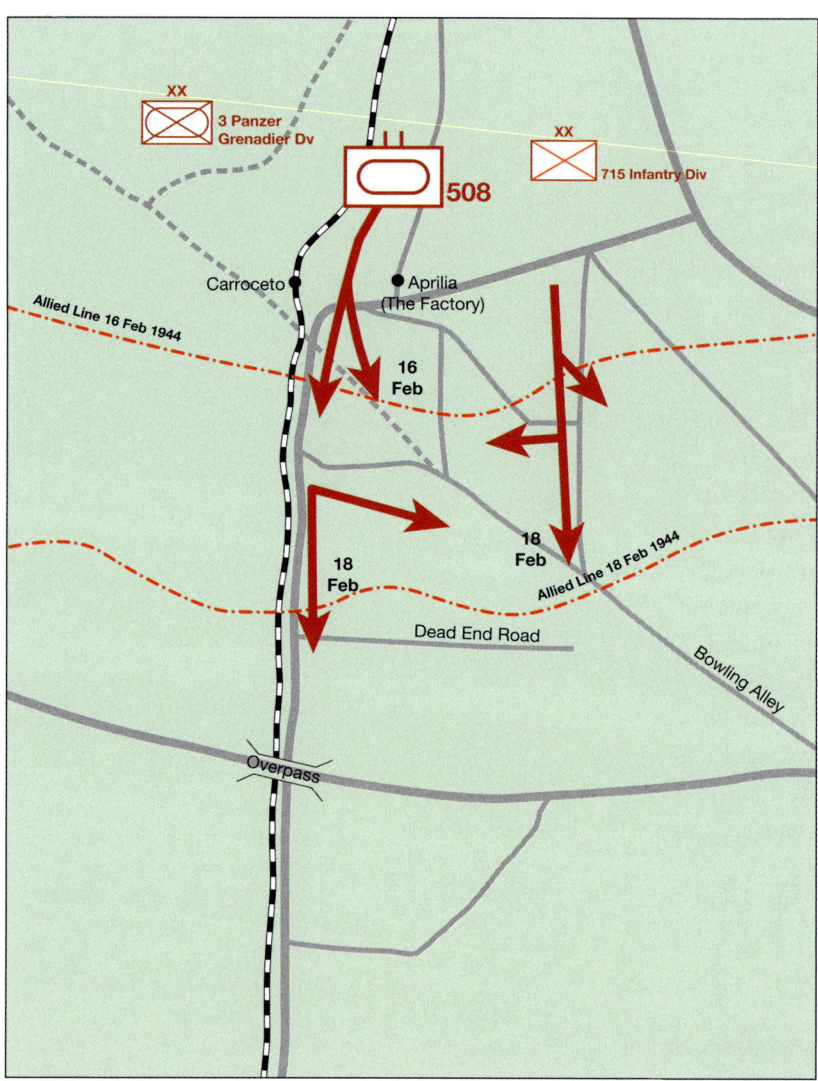

Calabria. German forces had been built up since the overthrow of Mussolini on July 25th and had moved swiftly to disarm the Italians when they announced their surrender in September. Thereafter it was essentially the Germans who oppose the Allied armies as they fought their way northward, Fifth Army in the west and Eighth Army in the east. By early October they had reached the line Volturno–Termoli. Winter rains and bitterly cold weather now set in and progress through the mountains was slow as they closed up on the Gustav Line, being mainly held up by the pivotal German position at Cassino. On January 22nd, 1944, in order to try to break the deadlock, the Allies mounted Operation Shingle to secure a beachhead at Anzio, behind the German lines. The landing was successful, but they were unable to break out of the beachhead.

While these operations were taking place the 504th was being reconstituted at the Wezep Training Area in Holland with Hauptmann

Friedrich Kühn in command. By the end of 1943/early 1944, the battalion was operational and, after training at Paderborn and then Parthenay (near Poitiers in France) with 16th SS Panzergrenadier Division, it once again entrained for Italy, crossing over the Brenner Pass on June 8th. It unloaded at Pontremoli, Sarzana and Massa stations, then set out on a long road march of some 90 miles to the front line, travelling mainly by night in order to avoid Allied aircraft. By this time, of course, the Allies had managed to break out of the beachhead, deal with Cassino, and capture Rome.

The 508th in Italy In addition to the 504th, the 508th had been sent to fight in Italy as part of the leading elements of the German assault on the Nettuno–Aprilia area of the Allied beachhead at Anzio. The 508th had been established at Heilbronn in July/August 1943, then transferred to Böblingen, then by rail to Mailly-le-Camp. The battalion was made up from personnel and vehicles of other Panzer units, including AFVs from various Funklenk companies. Major Helmut Hudel (*see Personalities*) took command on January 1st, 1944, and the unit moved by rail and road to Rome, then on toward Anzio, where it was initially attached to 26th Panzer Division. The battalion had a difficult journey, the railhead being some 125 miles from Anzio and the roads narrow and twisty. Some sixty percent of the Tigers suffered at

A 2nd Company, 508th, Tiger driving past the Victor Emmanuel II Monument in Rome on its way to the Anzio area. (*BA 310/880/38*)

least one breakdown during the journey, so the battalion arrived piecemeal instead of as a formed body. It was soon into action and thereafter took part in a number of attacks, the first being on February 16th from the area known as the Factory against American positions on Dead End and Lateral Roads.

All these attacks ended in failure, as did the final German assault to eliminate the beachhead that began on February 26th, due mainly to heavy and accurate naval gunfire supporting the beachhead troops. The stalemate continued until late May 1944, when the Allied troops, suitably reinforced, managed at last to break out. Now began the German withdrawal northward. However, before it began, the 508th was involved in an unsuccessful attempt to prevent the Anzio breakout linking up with a breakthrough the Gustav Line. Earlier, on March 3rd, 1944, it had absorbed the eight Tigers belonging to Heavy Tank

Italian campaign: movement and battles of Heavy Tank Battalions 504 and 508.

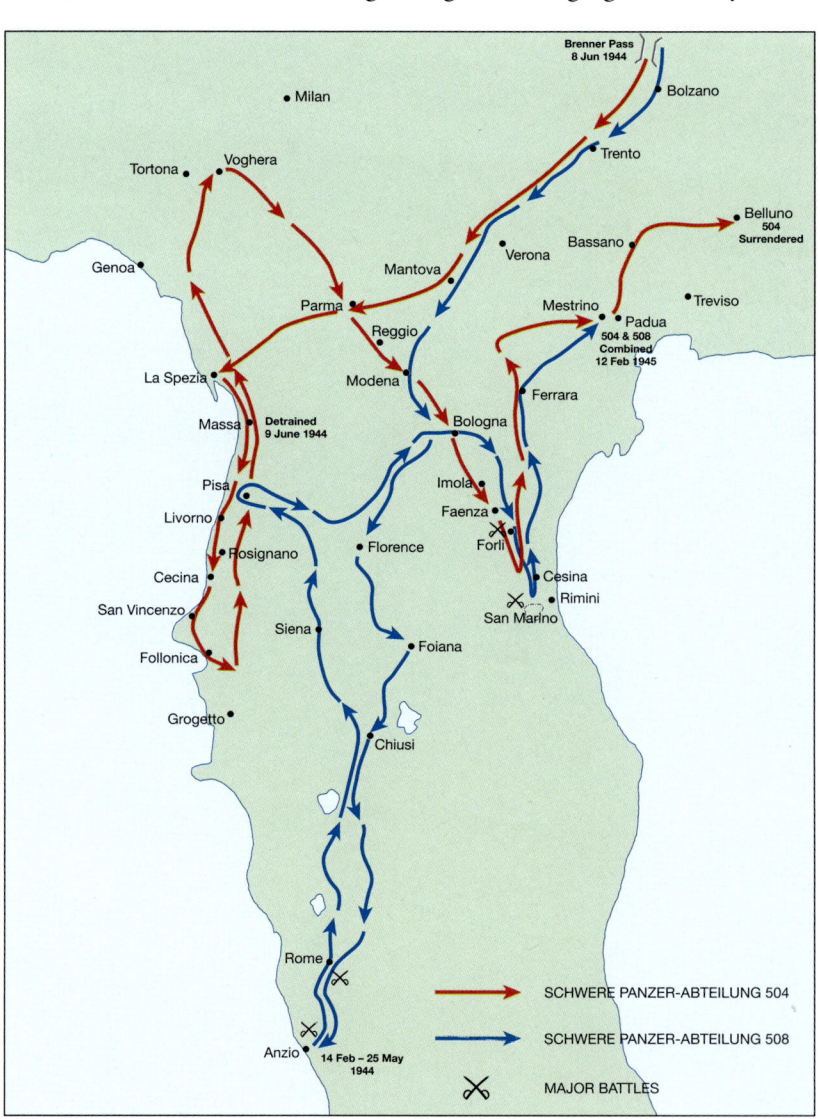

Another Tiger from 2nd Company, 508th, arriving in Rome on February 14th, 1944, after a long and difficult road journey for both vehicles and crews from the detraining station at Ficulle. The battalion was on its way to help contain the Allied beachhead at Anzio. Note the motorbike on the rear decks. *(BA 310/880/35)*

Company *Meyer*, which had been operating independently, Leutnant Meyer becoming the battalion adjutant

The 508th then assisted in covering the Axis withdrawal, first to Rome, then on up toward Bologna. By mid-February 1945, it was north of Cotignola, where it handed its remaining Tigers over to the 504th at San Filippo then gathered its personnel in the Padua area from whence the crews returned to Germany to train on Tiger IIs. However, few ever actually fought with the new tanks, the remainder being used as dismounted infantry in the Husen, Scherfelde and Hofgeismar areas, then later on near Berlin. They had knocked out over 100 enemy tanks while fighting in Italy.

The 504th Withdraws Meanwhile, by mid-June 1944, the 504th had become heavily involved in the withdrawal north of Rome. During a

A Tiger I from schwere Panzer-Kompanie *Meyer* encamped at the Brenner Pass on July 31st, 1943, after being taken by rail transport to Innsbruck and thence on its tracks. It would continue by road and rail down to the Anzio area. Later, on March 3rd, 1944, the company was integrated with s.Pz-Abt 508. *(Tank Museum 3663/E3)*

period of ten days, it would lose 28 of its 45 Tigers in a running battle with U.S. 1st Armored Division over some 120 miles of narrow, twisting, mountain roads. However, the vast majority of these casualties were not through being knocked out in combat. The going was such that many of the Tigers broke down or crashed and, before they could be repaired or recovered, were overrun by the lighter, faster-moving American armor. Christopher Wilbeck in *Sledgehammers* comments that in 40 days of action the two heavy tank battalions in Italy suffered 64 tank casualties, but that fewer than 5 of these were destroyed in combat, the remainder being breakdowns that subsequently had to be destroyed in order to avoid capture. He also comments that, for the majority of their combat time in Italy, the Tigers were never employed as a battalion, or even as a company or a platoon; instead they were spread out in "penny packets" or even as single tanks, violating General Guderian's principles as laid down in his manual. However, this did not always end in disaster, as time and again, a single machine or small group of Tigers proved quite capable of defending against heavy attacks, especially in the mountainous terrain.

After a period of being penny packeted—its tasks having included anti-partisan security in the wild Serchio Valley—on August 12th the 504th's companies were grouped together as a battalion under Marshal Graziani's Ligurian Army. After a short period in reserve, they were in action again around Rimini which was lost to the Allies on September

21st. Winter was once again closing in and, on December 20th, the 504th withdrew to the River Senio, which would remain the front line for the rest of the winter. On February 12th, 1945, as mentioned already, the 508th handed over its remaining tanks (fifteen Tigers and one Bergepanther) to the 504th at San Filippo.

Just over a week later, the 504th moved into reserve, but was soon in action again, when the Allied offensive began on April 9th. The battalion withdrew gradually toward the River Po, often under heavy fire and losing tanks both to the Allied fire and breakdowns. The last remaining Tiger had to be blown up by its crew on April 28th in the Piave Valley, having broken into an underground water pipe with one track. The remnants retired on foot to the Agordo Valley and it was there, on May 2nd, that they received the message that the German Army in Italy had capitulated. The following day they formally surrendered to U.S. forces at Belluno. The 504th had knocked out a total of over 270 enemy tanks (150 in Tunisia, 20 in Sicily and 100 in Italy) and one of its commanders had been awarded a Knight's Cross.

The Eastern Front

502nd—The First Battalion into Action The first heavy tank subunit was the 1st Platoon of the 502nd, and, as already explained, it was also the first operational subunit to be sent east, to the Leningrad area in

Operation Zitadelle. A crew from s.Pz-Abt 503 prepares for action. The 503rd Battalion was part of the attack by III Panzer Corps from Belgorod and destroyed many Soviet tanks. *(BA 22/2948/23)*

Tiger Is belonging to the 3rd Company of the 503rd moving up to the front line, August 13th, 1943. The number "13" stencilled on the underside of the commander's cupola refers to the 13th step in the procedure for sealing the tank prior to deep wading. (BA 751/801/22)

August 1942, under the unfortunate Major Märker. It then took part in various battles near Lake Ladoga, also in the Leningrad sector. By early 1943, it had only five of its original nine Tigers left, but had destroyed over 100 Russian tanks. After restructuring, the unit was made up to three companies and continued to fight on the Leningrad front, destroying many Soviet AFVs. From January 1944, the 502nd joined the German retreat from the Leningrad area and took part in the battle for the Narva bridgehead (February–April 1944), during which operation, on February 23rd, the battalion knocked out its 500th enemy tank (on September 26th, it would knock out the 1,000th). Operations were getting more and more difficult with the influx of heavier Soviet tanks and anti-tank guns like the new IS-2, with its powerful 122-mm gun. However, the battalion would remain in action on the northern sector of the Eastern Front for the rest of 1944. In 1945, now re-named as the 511th, it moved to East Prussia via Memel, where a Soviet offensive began in mid-January. Finally, near Nickelswalde, the battalion was disbanded and surrendered to the

Russians. However, some tanks went on fighting and eventually reached the southern slopes of the Harz mountains. The 502nd had knocked out over 1,400 enemy tanks and 2,000 anti-tank guns. No fewer than ten of its members were awarded Knight's Crosses, while two (Lieutenants Bölter and Carius) also received the Oak Leaves.

503rd—Next to Arrive on the Eastern Front This battalion was formed in early May 1942 at Neuruppin, under Oberstleutnant Post, from a nucleus of personnel from Panzer Regiments 5 and 6. Initially it could not be fully equipped with Tiger Is, so was brought up to strength with PzKpfw IIIs (Ausf N). It would fight to the bitter end both in the east and the west, first going to the southern sector of the Eastern Front, arriving in late December 1942 to join Army Group Don. It saw action during the attempted relief of Stalingrad, then in Operation Zitadelle at Kursk. At the start of 1944, the battalion was grouped with a Panther battalion from Panzer-Regiment 11, plus an artillery battalion, an engineer battalion and a mountain infantry battalion to form Panzer-Abteilung *Bäke*, commanded by Oberstleutnant (later Generalmajor) Franz Bäke. In a period of five days, the combination knocked out 267 Soviet tanks for the loss of just three Tigers and four Panthers, then spearheaded the attempt to free the Korsun-Cherkassy pocket. After being virtually decimated, the battalion was ordered to be re-formed in May 1944 at the Ohrdruf Training Area with a mixture of Tiger Is and Tiger IIs. In June it was sent to Normandy and finally to Hungary toward the end of December 1944, becoming known as the s.Pz-Abt *Feldherrnhalle* (due to the renaming of the three SS heavy tank battalions). Trapped in the Budapest area by the Red Army, it was all but annihilated, but the remnants managed to escape. Their last action was north of Vienna in mid-May 1945, trying to get to Bavaria but without success. It is recorded that the battalion knocked out a staggering 1,700 Allied tanks and 2,000 artillery guns, making it the most successful of all the heavy tank battalions. Four of its members were awarded Knight's Crosses, including Hauptmann Kageneck, who also won the Oak Leaves

The 505th Created on January 29th, 1943, at Fallingbostel, with Major Sauvant in command from February 20th, from elements of the 3rd and 26th Panzer Divisions for service in North Africa, it was then allocated first to the Eastern Front, then to the west. However, after some weeks of training at Beverlo, near Ghent in Belgium, it was finally deployed to the Eastern Front for service in the area of Orel, where it took part in operations with 2nd Panzer Division. These battles were followed by Operation Zitadelle and then fighting in the Orel, Dnieper and north Ukraine areas. Major Sauvant would be awarded the Oak

> **Multi-Purpose Weapon**
> The 8.8cm main gun on the Tiger tank was adapted from the 8.8-cm FlaK 36 anti-aircraft gun. The high velocity and flat trajectory of the "88" (as the Allies called it) made it ideal for both the ground-to-air and anti-armor role.

Leaves to his Knight's Cross on July 28th, 1943. The Tiger as always did well—for example in one action in September 1943, a single Tiger crushed an entire attack in the Smolensk area. In the summer of 1944, the battalion was re-equipped with Tiger IIs and in September 1944, moved by rail to Nasielsk, Poland, and was attached to Second Army as operational reserve. It was involved in the Narew sector, then in East Prussia (Goldap, Königsberg and Samland), its last actions being at Pillau. It surrendered at Peyse in mid-April 1945. The battalion had knocked out over 900 enemy tanks and some 1,000-plus anti-tank guns. Three members of the battalion were awarded Knight's Crosses, Major Sauvant, as already mentioned, winning the Oak Leaves.

The Re-Formed 501st Arriving on the Eastern Front in mid-December 1943, was the re-formed 501st. It would go on fighting on the Eastern Front until decimated by the Soviet offensive of early July 1944, being almost completely annihilated in the Minsk area while under command of Oberstleutnant von Legat, then Major Saemisch who was later killed in action. Yet again the battalion would be reconstituted at the Ohrdruf Training Area, where it would re-equip with Tiger IIs, and return to the Eastern Front, then fight in Poland and finally Germany. Re-designated as schwere Panzer-Abteilung 424 on December 21st, 1944, it was finally deactivated on February 11th, 1945. Most of the personnel were used to form Panzer-Jäger-Abteilung 512 at Detmold-Schöningen, equipped with Jagdtiger tank destroyers. What was left of the 3rd Company banded together with various tanks from the Armored Replacement and Training Battalion (Paderborn) and fought on until the last Tiger was knocked out and the remaining personnel surrendered at Höxter. The 501st/424th had destroyed some 450 enemy tanks—150 in North Africa, 200 in Russia with Tiger Is and 100 with Tiger IIs. Major Löwe was awarded both the Knight's Cross and Oak Leaves.

Heavy Tank Battalions at Kursk Just two heavy tank battalions took part in the German Kursk offensive (Operation Zitadelle). The 505th would play a pivotal role as part of the main breakthrough force in the northern arm of the massive pincer movement, designed to eliminate the Soviet salient around Kursk. The 503rd was initially employed with the force detailed to guard the flank of the southern arm of the pincer movement. (Oberst Bäke's daring part in the assault is covered in *Personalities*.) In order to do so, the corps commander attached one heavy tank company to each of his three divisions—directly contrary to General Guderian's guidance in the use of heavy tank battalions—and it was not until some days later that the 503rd's companies were reunited and it fought as a complete battalion.

Bigger and Bigger

The primary panzer in the German forces that invaded Poland on September 1st, 1939, was the PzKpfw II. The main gun for this tank was 20-mm caliber and the projectile weighed 0.35 pounds. Main gun for the Tiger II was 8.8-cm caliber and the projectile weighed 22.25lbs. The PzKpw II carried 180 main gun rounds as its standard combat load, the Tiger II's combat load included 92 main gun rounds.

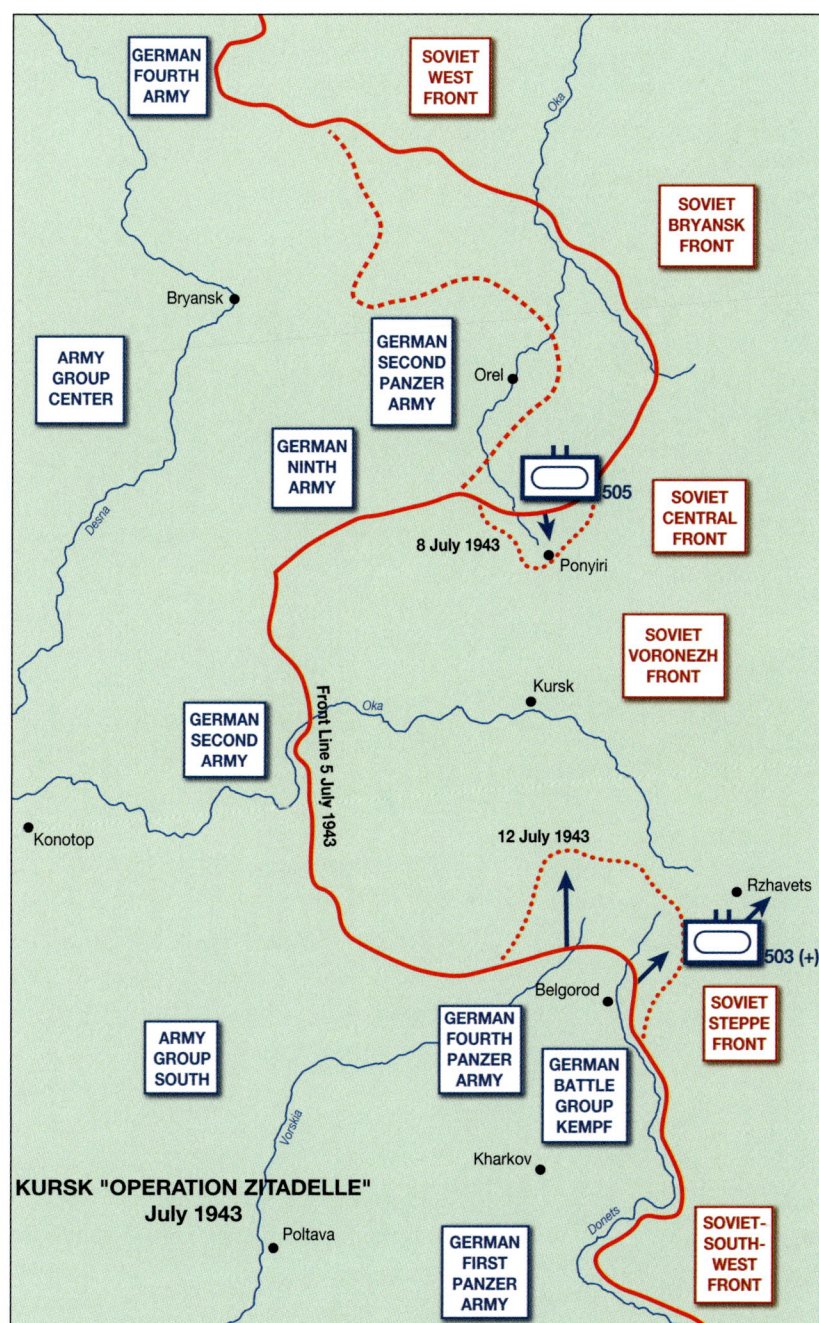

The Battle of Kursk, Operation Zitadelle, illustrating the parts played by s.Pz-Abt 503 and 505.

Zitadelle did not achieve its aim and its failure forced the Germans back onto the defensive. However, as far as the heavy tank battalions were concerned, despite not being used entirely as had been intended by Guderian, they had again shown that Tiger was an excellent "battering ram," that could withstand a considerable number of direct hits and still survive, at the same time knocking out large numbers of enemy tanks.

By the time of Kursk, as the production table on page 11 shows, Tiger production had steadily increased, so it was possible not only to

A Tiger I belonging to 3. Kompanie, s.Pz-Abt 502, pictured in the central area of the Eastern Front in late 1943. It is covered in mud and dust and over-painted with olive green on top of the original dark yellow base color. *(BA 457/56/12)*

replace those tanks lost in action, but also to make up all battalions to three companies. Additionally, the remaining heavy tank battalions were formed, so that by the summer of 1944 there were twelve in the Army (501–510, plus 3rd Battalion, *Grossdeutschland* Regiment and 301 [Funklenk]). The majority of these were employed on the Eastern Front with just the 504th and 508th in Italy.

Three More Battalions Arriving in the fall of 1943, the 3rd Battalion of Panzer Regiment *Grossdeutschland* together with 506th and 509th Heavy Tank Battalions were the next to fight on the Eastern Front and all three took part in the withdrawal that followed the failed Operation Zitadelle. Unfortunately this led to the loss of numerous broken-down Tigers that had to be left un-recovered on the battlefield, battalions being without the time they needed for maintenance or to repair battle damage. Tigers were also rapidly becoming victims of German propaganda (*see Assessment chapter*). However, this did not necessarily lessen their effectiveness as the actions in the Cherkassy pocket in early 1944 showed. For example, as detailed in the *Personalities* chapter, Heavy Regiment *Bäke* knocked out over 300 enemy tanks in just two months of fighting around Cherkassy, for the loss of just 22 Tigers.

Schwere Panzer-Abteilung *Grossdeutschland* (*GD*) had been established on the Sennelager Training Area under Major Gomille. It had begun as a single Tiger company in June 1943, but later became a full Tiger battalion and fought with this elite division for the rest of the war. Its first battle was in the Kharkov sector on the Eastern Front. In the spring of 1944, it was the first unit to fight against the new Soviet IS-2 heavy tank. *GD* continued to fight on the Eastern Front until April 1945, its tally being over 500 enemy tanks knocked out, while two of its members won Knight's Crosses.

The 506th had first been established at St Pölten, then moved to Sennelager for training under the command of Major Willing. Sent to Army Group South on the Eastern Front, it fought in the Zaporozhye bridgehead by the Dnieper River, and later near Stanislaw. In the summer of 1944 it handed over its Tiger Is to the 507th Heavy Tank Battalion and was re-equipped with Tiger IIs and sent west to help deal with the Allied airborne landings at Arnhem, then on to Germany—defending Geilenkirchen, Aachen, Eschweiler, and the Eifel—then into the Ardennes for operations near Bastogne. Finally it received some more Tiger IIs, fought in Germany, at Siegen east of Bonn and finally in the Ruhr, before being disbanded on April 14th, 1945. The 506th had knocked out over 400 enemy tanks (roughly 300 in Russia, 100 in the west) and one of its commanders was awarded the Knight's Cross.

Last of the three new arrivals was the 509th which had been first established at Schwetzingen in September 1943 under Hauptmann von Lüttich. Following training at Sennelager it then transferred to Mailly-le-Camp. In late October it was sent by rail to the southern part of the Eastern Front. However, difficulties were encountered toward the end of the journey as the Russians had cut the railway line. Having eventually completed the journey, it was heavily engaged in the

BELOW AND BELOW LEFT: Deep wading. The initial 495 production Tiger 1s were equipped for totally submerged wading to a depth of some 4 metres, with a snorkel breathing tube. However, this was an expensive luxury that was later discarded to simplify production. These photographs were taken just postwar at the experimental wading tank at Haustenbeck and show British officers watching Tiger 1 snorkelling. *(Barry Hook)*

A Tiger I, belonging to III./Panzer-Regiment *Grossdeutschland* passes some captured Russian artillery guns, in the fall of 1943, in the central part of the Eastern Front. *(BA 732/1381/14)*

Fastovetz–Sasslav–Kamenets Podolsky area in early 1944. At the end of the year it was withdrawn to be equipped with Tiger IIs, then in the spring of 1945 was moved to Hungary, to become both the local army reserve and the training battalion for Hungarian crews converting to the Tiger. It then fought in the same sector as 1st Panzer Division, making the long withdrawal to Kaplitz on the Moldau River, where the battalion surrendered to the Americans. The 509th had knocked out over 500 enemy tanks and three of its personnel received Knight's Crosses.

Two More Arrive These three heavy tank battalions would soon be followed by two more—the 507th in January 1944 and then, the last to be formed, the 510th in June 1944. The 507th was first established in Vienna in September 1943, under the command of Major Schmidt. It then moved to France to the Le Mans area for training that fall, then to Wezep in the Netherlands. Sent to the northern sector of the Eastern Front in early 1944, it was engaged in the Tarnopol–Brody area, then Baranovici–Ostrolenka. Withdrawal to the Warsaw–Danzig area followed. In March 1945, while still in the line, the battalion was re-equipped with a mixture of AFVs, including Tiger IIs and Hetzer tank destroyers. It continued to fight until May 12th, 1945, when it surrendered to an American force near Rosenthal, in a U.S. occupied area of Czechoslovakia. In its single year of combat the battalion had knocked out over 600 enemy tanks, while six of its members had received the Knight's Cross.

Finally, the last to be formed, the 510th, had been established at Paderborn on June 6th, 1944, under the command of Major Gilbert. On the 15th it had moved to Ohrdruf, where on July 1st it was inspected by General Guderian. It was then rushed to the central sector of the Eastern Front to help try to stop the Soviet summer offensive. It was first committed south of Kovno, then later moved to East Prussia and then to the Courland area in Latvia/Lithuania. The battalion would

A Tiger I belonging to III. Abteilung, Panzer Regiment *Grossdeutschland*, loaded on a train bound for Romania in 1944. Note that the Tiger has been fitted with the narrower transport tracks which will have to be taken off and replaced with normal-width tracks when the journey is over. The crew will sleep in the pup tent made by combining a number of *Zeltbahnen* (waterproof shelter triangles) made from closely woven water-repellent cotton and issued universally throughout the German Army. *(BA 7321/1331/34)*

Romania 1944. The narrower transport tracks are in the process of being changed now that they have reached their destination. Note the *GD* helmet tactical sign on the roadsign to the rear of the photograph. *(BA 732/133/13)*

The Soviet advance into Germany and the approximate operational areas of the heavy tank battalions which served on the Eastern Front.

surrender to Allied troops in April 1945, near Putlos. In under a year of operations, the 510th knocked out 200 enemy tanks, its CO and a company commander receiving the Knight's Cross.

All the Tiger units were constantly on operations and had to defend over wide frontages, on many occasions without supporting infantry, and deal with the recovery of damaged and broken-down vehicles during

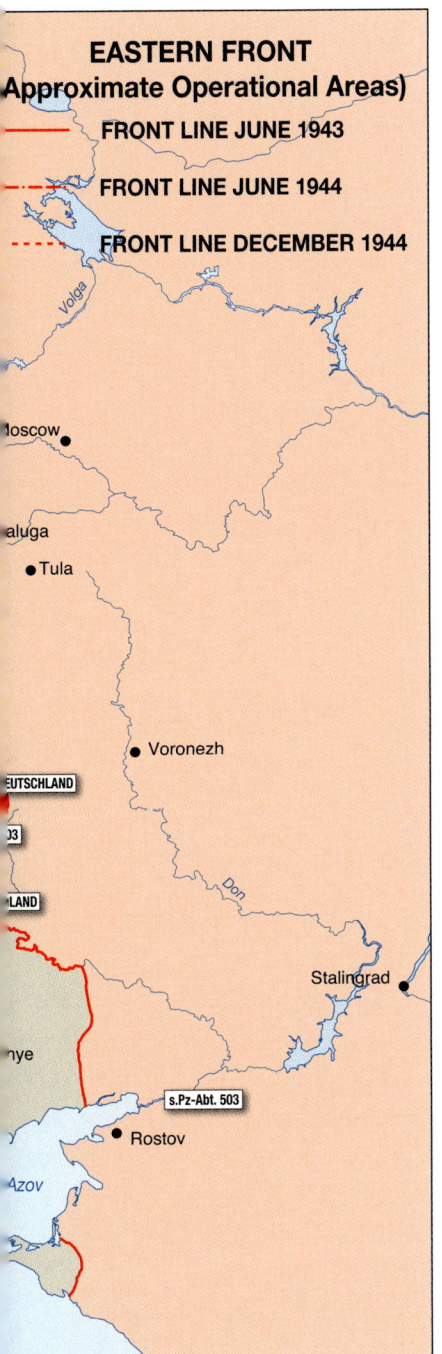

EASTERN FRONT
(Approximate Operational Areas)

—— FRONT LINE JUNE 1943

—·— FRONT LINE JUNE 1944

-·-·- FRONT LINE DECEMBER 1944

Tanks of s.Pz-Abt 506 advancing to attack Tarnopol in April 1944. Each tank is carrying two 200-liter (53 U.S. gal.) fuel drums that will be jettisoned when empty. Note also that the tank second from the rear is a Befehlswagen (command tank) with tubes for holding spare aerial rods on its rear. *(Compendium)*

difficult withdrawal scenarios, especially those involving water obstacles and weak bridges. Another common experience among these battalions was for elements of the heavy tank battalion (even single Tigers) to be flung into battle as and when they arrived and not given a chance to concentrate into a formed unit.

Operation Bagration The main summer offensive of 1944 by Soviet forces began on the morning of June 22nd, three years to the day after the original German attack on the U.S.S.R. The aim of Bagration was to destroy the German Army Group Center and it was helped by the fact that, only two weeks before, the Germans had had to transfer units to Normandy to meet the Allied D-Day invasion. Four Soviet army groups, totalling over 120 divisions, smashed into the thinly held German line. The Russians had overwhelming resources, having, for example, achieved a ten to one superiority in tanks at the points of attack. In ten days they had broken through the German defenses and reached the old Polish border. When the attack began only one heavy tank battalion was part of Army Group

OPPOSITE: Northern Russia in the late fall of 1943. A well-spaced column of Tigers belonging to SS Panzer-Regiment 2 move through a forest shrouded in the early autumnal snow. (BA 571/721/31)

PAGES 60–61, MAIN PICTURE: Entry into Budapest. Once inside the city, the wide thoroughfares were mainly unblocked and, as can be seen, this Tiger II was able to move about more easily. Note its Henschel turret. Photograph taken October 16th, 1944. (BA 680/8282a/38a)

PAGES 60–61, INSET: Two Tiger II crew members (driver on left side of tank) both wearing their radio headsets and the regulation black Panzer uniform, with the black peaked Einheitsfeldmütze cap. The photograph was taken in Budapest in October 1944; the tank belonged to s.Pz-Abt 503. (BA 680/8282A/9)

Center, the 501st, which, as mentioned already, had been re-formed after being wiped out in Tunisia in 1943, then loaded at Mailly-le-Camp in December 1943. The battalion was taken by rail to Bialystok, unloaded there, and was immediately involved in heavy fighting in the Vitebsk area north-east of Minsk, where it destroyed 81 enemy tanks in five days for the loss of just four Tigers. However, by July 5th, 1944, all its Tigers had either been knocked out or handed over to other heavy tank battalions, and the battalion was withdrawn to be re-equipped, on the Führer's orders, with Tiger IIs for operations in the west.

Meanwhile, OKH had assigned four heavy tank battalions (the 505th, 506th, 507th, and 509th) to Army Group North, where clever Russian misinformation had persuaded them that the main assault would be aimed. However, when it was appreciated that Army Group Center was to be the focus of the enemy attack, two battalions (505th and 507th) were taken by rail and employed as blocking forces in the Borisov area. As always they knocked out many Soviet tanks, achieving a high kill ratio and, at the same time, held the withdrawal routes open to allow other German units to escape. Eventually they would be withdrawn back to Germany, to be re-equipped with Tiger IIs.

On into Poland The Soviet forces did not stop their offensive at the Polish border, but continued, reaching the River Vistula in early August and establishing a series of small bridgeheads across. Indeed, it was much the same situation on the other fronts too. It was in defense of two small bridgeheads in the Sandomierz and Baronovo areas on the Vistula River that 501st Heavy Tank Battalion, now equipped with Tiger IIs, would first use its new tanks in battle. It had already experienced major mechanical problems with the new tanks and in the battles to deal with the incursions would find itself up against the new Soviet heavy tank, the IS-2, which proved far more maneuverable than the almost roadbound Tiger II, leading to heavy German losses.

Hungary As well as battles in Poland, heavy tank battalions were involved in Hungary, where the re-equipped 503rd (now with some 45 Tiger IIs) was sent in mid-October 1944, arriving in Budapest on October 13th/14th, 1944. Its first task was to help in suppressing a coup that had been mounted by the Regent, Admiral Horthy, whose relations with Hitler had been deteriorating since 1943, when he had asked that Hungarian troops be withdrawn from the Eastern Front. Hitler had reacted by sending German troops to occupy Hungary in March 1944. The stalemate continued until the Russians were within 50 miles of Budapest in October 1944, when Horthy undertook to conclude a separate peace treaty with them, which failed. Having done its job (merely by taking up key positions around the city, the sheer bulk

A Tiger II of s.Pz-Abt 503 negotiates rubble-strewn streets on its way into Budapest, October 1944. *(BA 680/8282a)*

of the Tiger IIs having a salutary effect upon the locals), the battalion was ordered out of the city to take part in operations elsewhere, being heavily involved in stopping a Russian attack in the Lake Balaton area in December 1944.

Normandy

Waffen-SS Battalions The Waffen-SS received some of the first Tiger tanks—the elite *Leibstandarte Adolf Hitler*, *Totenkopf* and *Das Reich* Divisions were all allocated sufficient Tiger Is in late 1942 to enable them each to field a Tiger company. They saw action on the Eastern Front throughout the following year, but it was not until well into 1943 that the first of the full SS heavy tank battalions came into being. First of these was the 101. SS schwere Panzer-Abteilung (later to be re-designated as the 501st) that was established at the Sennelager Training Area on July 19th, 1943, under SS-Sturmbannführer von Western-hagen. Part of this new battalion comprised tank crews from the heavy companies of *LAH* and *Das Reich*. After formation and live-firing exercises it would be sent to Normandy. Much the same happened with the 102. SS schwere Panzer-Abteilung (later redesignated as the 502nd), which was established at Sennelager also on July 19th, 1943 under SS-Sturmbannführer Lackmann. It was transported to France by rail, then redeployed to the Wezep Training Area in the Netherlands. It would also fight in Normandy. The third SS heavy tank battalion, the 103rd under SS-Sturmbannführer Paetsch, was established in the spring of 1944 as corps troops for III. (germanisches) SS Panzerkorps in

Tiger Is, newly arrived at their unit from the factory, carry out low-level, tactical maneuvers in France in late April 1943, prior to a unit move to Russia. Note the splendid château in the background. *(BA 28/1609/16a)*

Paderborn. It would redeploy to Kampen, near Zwolle in the Netherlands, then to Epe with SS-Obersturmbannführer Leiner now in command. It would not go to Normandy, but rather retrain on Tiger IIs, after being redesignated SS schwere Panzer-Abteilung 503 on November 14th, 1944, then sent by rail to the Eastern Front

Normandy Only one Army heavy tank battalion (503rd) would see operational service in Normandy, plus two of the Waffen-SS heavy tank battalions (101st and 102nd), the 503rd being attached to 21st Panzer Division, while the latter two battalions went to I and II SS Panzerkorps respectively. One of the companies of the 503rd had just been re-equipped with Tiger IIs (June 11th–17th), the first operational tank company to be so re-equipped, while the other two companies received new Tiger Is. All would be involved against the British forces in the Caen area, so both types of Tiger would have battles against a rather more worthy opponent than previously, namely the Sherman Firefly. Two of the battalions—the Army 503rd and the Waffen-SS 102nd—would also experience considerable problems from Allied air attacks during their respective road journeys to Normandy, rail travel only being possible as far as Paris, because of course the Allies had complete air superiority over France. The 503rd would see action in the Colombelles area, but in September 1944 return to Germany to be fully re-equipped with Tiger IIs, renamed s.Pz-Abt *Feldherrnhalle*, and prepared for its part in Hitler's surprise Wacht Am Rhein offensive in the Ardennes.

After a difficult road journey from its training area, the 101st was remarkably successful initially, thanks to the bravery and quick-wittedness of one of its commanders, SS-Obersturmführer Michael Wittmann, whose action at Villers-Bocage (*see Personalities chapter*) put an end to the British 7th Armoured Division's daring right hook around the Panzer Lehr Division, which, had it succeeded, might have proved fatal to the German defense of Normandy. While Wittmann's single-handed attack stopped the British advance guard in its tracks, the subsequent actions of his understrength heavy tank battalion, with some assistance from the Panzer Lehr Division, put paid to the Allied capture of Villers-Bocage and compelled the British force to withdraw. However, although this was the initial outcome, in the long term perhaps the Germans would suffer more than the Allies—the Germans losing a number of Tiger tanks that could not be replaced, while the Allies had many more replacement tanks in the pipeline, ready to take the place of those lost by 4th County of London Yeomanry (4 CLY).

This Axis success was almost immediately followed by a series of actions that stressed the importance of air superiority and depleted the German armor by heavy bombing. Although the Allied Goodwood and

OPPOSITE: August 1944, replenishment in progress. The crew of this Tiger I, belonging to s.Pz-Abt 510, the very last heavy tank battalion sent to the Eastern Front, are all busy refuelling and "bombing up." *(BA 78/107/6)*

PAGES 66–67, MAIN PICTURE: These Tiger Is of the SS Panzerkorps *Leibstandarte* are on their way to Normandy soon after D-Day. They were photographed about June 10th some miles east of Rouen, crews keeping a watchful eye out for Allied *Jabos* (fighter-bombers). They belong to tank ace SS-Obersturmführer Michael Wittmann's company in SS s.Pz-Abt 101, soon to give battle at Villers-Bocage. *(BA 299/1804/11)*

PAGES 66–67, INSET LEFT: This Tiger I was photographed on June 14th, 1944, just after the battle at Villers-Bocage had ended. Note the cross keys insignia on the right-hand side of the front plate. The tank is towing another Tiger away from the village and there is strong evidence to suggest that the tank being towed is the one which Wittmann commanded during the battle. *(BA 238/267/18)*

PAGES 66–67, INSET RIGHT: France, June 1944. The only heavy tank battalion to arrive in the Normandy area to meet the Allied landings was s.Pz-Abt 503, which had been newly equipped with some Tiger IIs. However, it was attacked by Allied aircraft en route and suffered badly. Here two Tiger IIs take cover from aerial view under a strip of woodland. *(BA 721/359/37)*

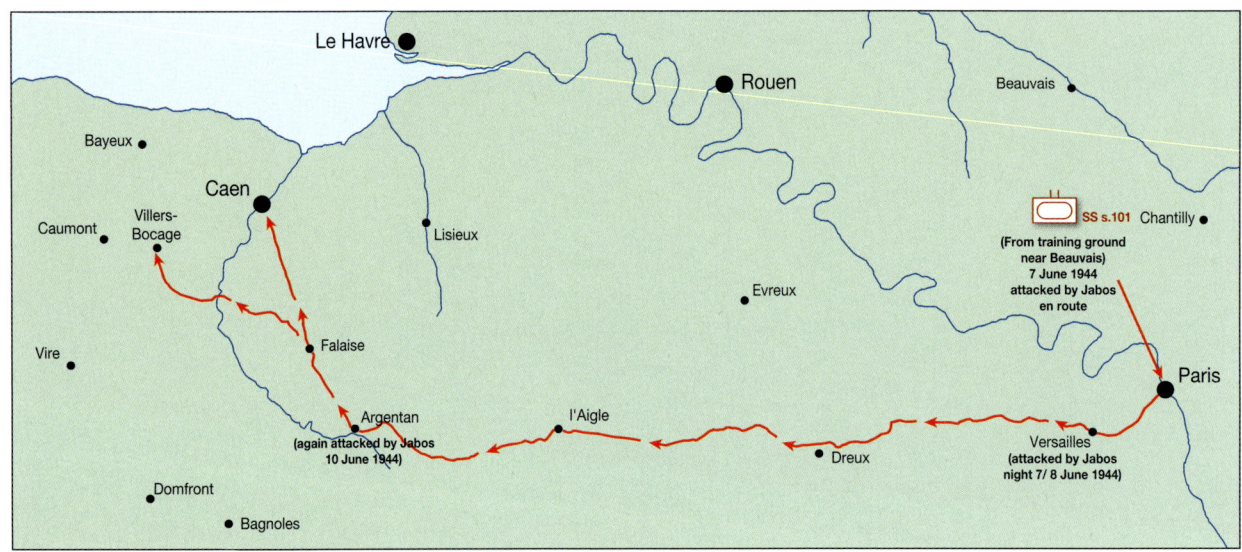

France 1944. The route to Normandy of SS s.Pz-Abt 501, June 7th–13th, 1944.

Bluecoat assaults did not break through the German defenses, they did serve to deplete the German forces even more seriously, especially their armor. However, as on so many other occasions, the heavy tank battalions, in particular, the SS 102nd, destroyed large numbers of Allied AFVs. Nevertheless, by early August 1944, the situation for the German forces was desperate and Operation Totalize—a Canadian/Polish breakout from the main Normandy beachhead area—joined the advance of U.S. Third Army in trapping German forces in what became known as the Falaise Pocket. These actions would see the demise of much German armor including the redoubtable Michael Wittmann,

Operation Market Garden The 506th Heavy Tank Battalion was reorganized and re-equipped with Tiger IIs in August 1944 at Ohrdruf, and toward the end of September (22nd–24th), would be sent to the Arnhem area in order to help to take on the daring Allied airborne landings and block the attempt to capture the bridge there over the Lower Rhine. The 506th was the only heavy tank battalion involved at Arnhem; however, so was the independent Heavy Tank Company *Hummel* (from Paderborn on attachment to 10th SS Panzer Division). All its tanks except two, broke down during the long approach march and the two remaining were knocked out by British PIATs (Projector Infantry Anti-Tank). The following month the 506th would entrain once again to assist in relieving Aachen. Later, in mid-December, it would be moved to the Eifel, to be involved in the Ardennes.

Too Thinly Spread Everywhere on every front, the German Army in general, and the heavy tank battalions in particular, were all too thinly spread. Indeed this stage of the war is perhaps a useful time at which to examine their battlefield "spread." In the east, there were three battalions in Poland, two in the north withdrawing stubbornly under continuous Soviet pressure, while the other endeavored to stop further enemy progress over the Vistula. Three more had retreated from Normandy, much whittled down by the fighting there. Two were in Italy, withdrawing before continuous Allied pressure, to the area north of the Gothic Line. Three more were in Lithuania and Latvia, trying to prevent further Soviet advances. The remaining four were in Germany at the Ohrdruf Training Area, converting to Tiger II and/or preparing to defend the Fatherland.

The Battle of the Bulge

Although in many ways the Tiger II was better than its predecessor, there were still plenty of teething troubles to be overcome which did not

The retreat from northern France. Photographed in the small French town of Bourgtheroulde on August 12th, 1944, this Tiger I belonging to s.Pz-Abt 503 was withdrawing in front of Allied pressure and making for Elbouef to cross the Seine. *(BA 301/1951/24)*

make its crews' lives any easier, so all in all it seems to have been an extremely difficult time to launch a major assault like Wacht Am Rhein, Hitler's daring attack on the Allied defenses in the Ardennes, which began on December 16th, 1944, and was designed not just to rupture the Allied front, but to break through all the way to the sea. Eleven tank and fourteen infantry divisions would attempt to smash their way through six weak American divisions along a 60-mile front from Monschau in Belgium to Echternach in Luxembourg.

Two heavy tank battalions, both equipped with Tiger IIs, were part of the attacking force—the SS 501st and the Army 506th. The former was an integral part of the leading combat team of I SS Panzerkorps of Sixth Panzer Army, named Kampfgruppe *Peiper* after its commander.

Given the task of spearheading the assault for Sixth Panzer Army, Peiper quickly realized that the Tiger II was entirely wrong for the job, being too slow and unreliable mechanically. It was also totally unsuited to the bad weather conditions of the winter and the obvious lack of good, well-surfaced roads. Therefore he put the heavy tank battalion (45 Tiger IIs) at the rear of his combat team column. The Tiger IIs were plagued by continual breakdowns and the first to suffer from enemy action was attacked by U.S. Republic P 47 Thunderbolts. These single-seat fighter-bombers attacked the column and damaged a Tiger but did not knock it out. However, it was never repaired, so eventually it had to be abandoned.

As one can imagine, the continual breakdowns caused the column to fragment and led to large gaps between vehicles. After the head of the column had passed through Stavelot, the Allied forces blocked the road,

An Expensive Luxury?

"Tiger took 300,000 man-hours to build and cost 800,000 Reichsmarks per tank, so critics were not slow to point out that two Panthers could be built in the same number of man-hours as one Tiger, while three Messerschmitt Bf 109 fighters cost the equivalent of one Tiger."

From: *German Tanks of World War Two*, George Forty

after dealing with the small detachment Peiper had left there. Only six Tiger IIs had managed to get through Stavelot and on toward La Gleize (where there is still a knocked out Tiger II to be seen at the roadside). For five days from December 19th, 1944, the Tigers defended against numerous counter-attacks by U.S. 30th Infantry and 3rd Armored Divisions, despite being short of fuel, ammunition and supplies. In the end it was decided to scuttle the vehicles and for the crews to break out on foot.

The other heavy tank battalion (506th) was in the Eifel region endeavoring to help encircle the U.S. 106th Infantry Division which

Disturbing a placid farmyard scene. This Tiger I, on maneuvers in France, looks somewhat out of place as it passes cows on their way to be milked. It is still in its factory paint job of dark yellow overall. *(BA 28/1607/26)*

This Tiger II from SS s.Pz-Abt 501 was part of Kampfgruppe *Peiper* and was photographed here halfway between Malmédy and St Vith. Four paratroopers are hitching a ride as 1st SS Panzer Division presses on. *(U.S. Army)*

was defending that area. It managed not only to prevent the U.S. forces from withdrawing toward St Vith, but also broke through the American lines there and forced them to retreat from the town.

Despite these limited successes it would on balance be fair to say that the two heavy tank battalions contributed very little to Wacht am Rhein, their vehicles being too large and cumbersome, too prone to breakdowns, and too thirsty, producing a fuel supply problem. Casualties were estimated at 25 Tiger IIs between the two battalions, most of which were breakdowns/scuttling by crews rather than enemy action.

Heavy Tank Battalion 301 (Funklenk) Also in action in the area between the Ardennes in Luxembourg and Cologne in Germany, during the period from November 1944 until almost the end of the war, was the heavy tank battalion s.Pz-Abt 301 (Funklenk). It had been re-equipped in October 1944 with 31 Tiger Is with which to operate its Borgward B IV remotely controlled demolition carriers. By mid-April 1945, when the battalion scuttled its last three remaining Tigers near Sprockhövel in the Ruhr bridge area, it had destroyed some 60–70 Allied tanks.

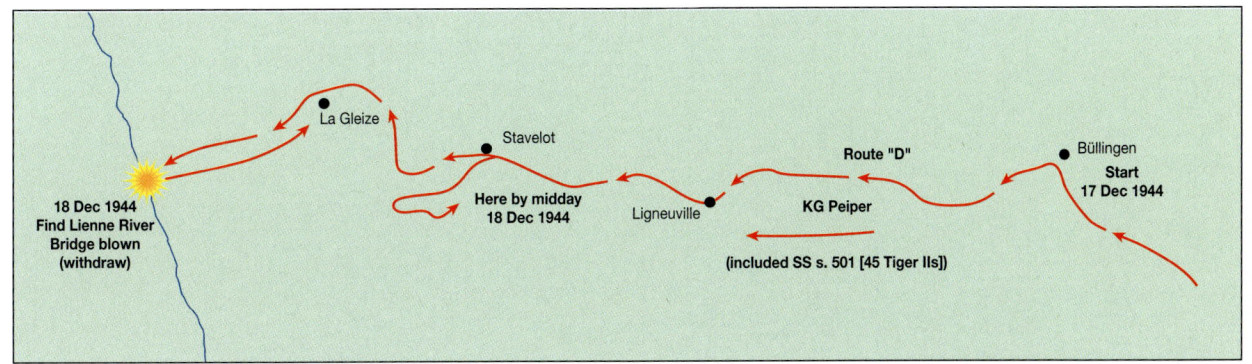

La Gleize

Stavelot

Route "D"

Büllingen
Start
17 Dec 1944

18 Dec 1944
Find Lienne River
Bridge blown
(withdraw)

Here by midday
18 Dec 1944

Ligneuville

KG Peiper

(included SS s. 501 [45 Tiger IIs])

Battle of the Bulge. The advance by
Kampfgruppe *Peiper* at the start of the
German offensive.

Wacht am Rhein had cost the Allies a delay of some six weeks and over 75,000 casualties, but the cost to Germany was far greater—100,000 casualties and over 800 irreplaceable tanks and other AFVs. This failure had also undoubtedly hastened the final defeat of Germany and thus the complete destruction of the *Panzerwaffe*.

To the Oder

On the morning of January 12th, 1945, the Soviet armies launched their largest offensive of the war, aimed at the very heart of Germany with the ultimate objective to capture Berlin. Along the entire front from the Baltic to the Carpathians, no fewer than five army groups moved forward and the Germans, hopelessly outnumbered, could do nothing but fall back in front of such pressure. However, instead of concentrating his forces on defending the Oder, Hitler chose to counter-attack through Hungary, aiming to throw the Red Army back across the Danube and relieve Budapest. He took no notice of his experts, firing his armored guru, Heinz Guderian, on March 21st, for example. For the heavy tank battalions, as for the rest of the German forces, this stupid counter-attack directly led to the disintegration of their supply systems as fuel, ammunition, spare parts, rations, and all the rest dried up.

Four heavy tank battalions were involved in the operations in Hungary: the 424th (ex-501st), *Feldherrnhalle* (ex-503rd), the 509th and the SS 501st (ex-101st). What was left of these severely depleted battalions, retreated, maintaining order as best they could, into Austria and Czechoslovakia, aiming to get as far westward as possible, so as to be able to surrender to the Western Allies before the Red Army could catch up with them.

Other battalions like III./GD, the 502nd, SS 503rd, and 507th, which had been fighting further north, made for northern Germany, East Prussia and Poland, while the 510th, the last Tiger I battalion to be formed, that had been rushed to the east to help try to stop Bagration, had gone on fighting against the Red Army as part of Army Group North, so had no option but to surrender to the Russians.

s.Pz-Abt Locations, Mid-January 1945	
501st/424th	Southern Poland
502nd/511th	Latvia
503rd/*Feld'halle*	Hungary
504th	Northern Italy
505th	Lithuania
506th	Western Germany
507th	Poland
508th	Northern Italy
509th	Hungary
510th	Latvia
III./GD	Northern Poland
301st (Fl)	Germany
SS 501st	Hungary
SS 502nd	Germany
SS 503rd	Germany

Formed up and ready to start. Fortunately only 489 Tiger IIs were ever built, so they did little to stop the flood of Allied armor despite being able to eliminate all opponents with ease. *(BA 75/102/14A)*

"Ein Wunderwerk!" (a marvel) is how the original caption describes this column of Tiger IIs, belonging to 3. Kompanie, s.Pz-Abt 503, as they motor toward the location of a propaganda film. *(BA 75/102/12A)*

Defending the Fatherland In the last few months of the war in Europe, both on the Eastern and Western Fronts, the heavy tank battalions were virtually completely destroyed and their crews taken into captivity. Numbers of active Tigers naturally got less and less as the battle casualties and breakdowns mounted and the resupply chain became more and more fragmented, as the Allies pressed remorselessly onward toward the very heart of the Fatherland.

Two heavy tank battalions—the 504th and 508th—were in Italy being pushed further and further northward. Some of their personnel would escape into Austria and finally surrender to the Americans, while the 506th, which had fought in the Battle of the Bulge in the Ardennes, would be one of the few battalions to reach and fight in western Germany, before surrendering to the Americans. Two other battalions would participate in the fighting around the German capital—the Waffen-SS 502nd and 503rd. These were fragmented but still destroyed significant numbers of enemy tanks even during the last few days of conflict.

Individually Attached Tigers

While this summary has concentrated on the heavy tank battalions of the German Army and the Waffen-SS, there were at times other Tigers in other units and subunits within the German armed forces, although mainly in relatively small numbers. These naturally included units that were part of the training system, located, for example, at the establishments used for Tiger training, armor experimentation, and instruction.

There were also two heavy Panzer companies formed in the fall of 1944: schwere Panzer-Kompanie *Hummel* and s.Pz-Kp *Meyer*. The former (from Paderborn with fourteen Tiger Is) saw action in the Arnhem area during September 1944, then later in the Eifel Mountains and then, in February 1945, saw combat against the first U.S. Army Pershings to be shipped to north-west Europe. This included the first tank-versus-tank battle between Tiger I and Pershing, with first blood going to the Tiger, after a Pershing was knocked out at close range. However, not long afterward the GIs got their own back and knocked out a Tiger I again at fairly close range (*see Assessment chapter*). Kompanie *Meyer*, equipped with eight Tiger Is, was formed in July 1943, moved by rail to Innsbruck, then across the Brenner Pass to assist in the disarmament of Italian troops after Italy capitulated. Then, it moved to Rome and, in January 1944, was involved against the Allied landing at Anzio. Finally in March 1945, it was consolidated with s.Pz-Abt 508 near Cisterna.

A few other operational units had Tigers. For example, in June 1944, Panzer Lehr's 130th Panzer Regiment had three Tiger Is in its establishment. A number of *ad hoc* units were also formed toward the end of the war, in vain last-ditch attempts to protect a particular part of the Fatherland. These included ex-training tanks—for example at Paderborn, where eighteen training Tiger Is and nine training Tiger IIs,

Other Tiger Units

Wolfgang Schneider lists the following formations and units as having had individually attached Tigers during the war:

Armor School at Bergen-Hohne
Panzer Division *Clausewitz*
Tiger-Gruppe *Fehrmann*
Fallschirm-Panzer-Korps *Hermann Göring*
Panzer-Kompanie *Kummersdorf*
Panzer-Grenadier-Division *Kurmark*
Panzer-Abteilung *Kummersdorf/ Müncheberg*
Panzerkampfgruppe *Nord*
Panzer-Kompanie *Paderborn*
Panzergruppe *Paderborn*
Panzer-Kompanie *Panther*
Panzer Lehr Division
Panzer Lehr Abteilung Putlos
The Fortress of Putlos
Tigers in Slovakia

Source: Schneider, *Tigers in Combat*

Got a light? A paratrooper passes a light to a despatch rider from the back decks of this massive Tiger II. There was always plenty of room for hitchhikers until the tank had to go into action. (*U.S. Army*)

helped form a Kampfgruppe for operations in the local area between March 30th and April 12th, 1945.

Most saw action in the last weeks of the war, while desperately trying to defend their corner of the Fatherland, and at the same time ensure that when the time came to surrender that it was to the Western Allies and not the dreaded Red Army. Not all managed to do so.

So ended the war for the heavy tank battalions. Their reputation and that of the Tiger tank would live on.

EQUIPMENT & INSIGNIA

The Balkankreuz and the Swastika

Although its position varied, all German tanks normally bore the black, edged in white, national symbol of the *Balkankreuz*, somewhere on the turret or bodywork. The usual place was on the center of either the hull or turret sides. The Nazi Swastika does not appear to have been painted on any German tanks, although the national flag in which the black swastika appeared in a white disc on a red field, was often used as an air recognition sign, draped, for example, over the turret. However, this was only common in areas where the Germans had air superiority, so by the time the heavy tank battalions were operating on the Western Front it was rarely if ever used.

Some units, as seen on this this Tiger I belonging to SS s.Pz-Abt 101, set a very high standard of camouflage painting—even though it has posed in front of a church. Tiger 131 was commanded by SS-Hauptsturmführer Möbius, commander of the 1st Company. *(BA 299/1804/4)*

Turret Numbering

The German armed forces used a standardized form of turret numbering, each tank being allocated a three digit number, say for example: "213." The first digit indicated the company the tank belonged to, the second the platoon and the last, the vehicle's seniority within the platoon. So, 213 stands for the third tank, of the 1st platoon of the 2nd company. This system did have variations and within the heavy tank battalions sometimes the prefix "s" was added. At right, by way of example, are the initial turret numbers allocated to the tanks of 501. s.Pz-Abt:

This Tiger I, photographed in Russia in the spring of 1944, belonged to s.Pz-Abt 505. Note the charging knight unit sign on the side of the turret, while the turret number (312) is boldly painted on the armored recoil guard. Note also the new steel-tired, rubber-cushioned, roadwheels. *(BA 90/947/16)*

Tigers:
Company HQ and platoons of 1st Company: 100, 101, 111, 112, 121, 122, 131, 132, 141, 142
Battalion HQ: 01, 02
2nd Company (in France): 200, 201, 211, 212, 221, 222, 231, 232, 241, 242

PzKpfw III:
In platoons: 113, 114, 123, 124, 133, 134, 143 and 144
Concentrated in light platoon: 03, 04, 05, 06, 07, 08, 09, 10

Camouflage was essential, especially in north-west Europe where the Allies had overwhelming air superiority. This Tiger crew from SS Panzerkorps *Leibstandarte* have cut plenty of branches but will still have to do something about hiding the gun barrel. *(BA 738/275/10)*

Unit Insignia

All s.Pz-Abt had individual battalion insignia as the drawings show, although in some cases the insignia might be varied when either the unit was serving in a certain area, or had been re-constituted after being disbanded/destroyed in action. This was also sometimes resorted to in order to confuse Allied intelligence. The unit insignia were sometimes painted on the tank but, like the *Balkankreuz*, the location varied. Some units never seem to have painted their battalion symbols on their tanks, but did put them on supporting vehicles and on their roadsigns/bivouac area signs. Toward the end of the war, the Army High Command ordered all such unit insignia to be painted out for security reasons.

As will be seen from the drawings, the 501st chose a stalking Tiger as its unit sign; the 502nd selected a mammoth; the 503rd chose a Tiger's head looking to the left; the 504th went for the parallelogram that represented tank units in German organizational charts (including a stripe to denote a "heavy" tank unit); and the 505th selected a mounted knight charging. These last two battalions also used another symbol at various times in their existence; for the former the parallelogram contained a curling section of tank track pierced with a lance; while, in the latter's case, the symbol was a shield containing both the mounted knight and a snorting, charging bull. The other five heavy tank battalions chose very differing symbols as can be seen. The 506th

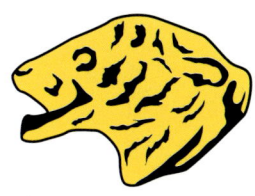

Schwere Panzer-Abteilung 501.
Insignia used in North Africa in
1942–3.

Schwere Panzer-Abteilung 502.
Insignia seen in the Leningrad area in
late 1942.

Schwere Panzer-Abteilung 503.
Insignia used in the Belgorod area in
the summer of 1943.

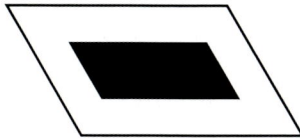

Schwere Panzer-Abteilung 504.
Insignia used by the battalion from its
creation to the end of the war.

Schwere Panzer-Abteilung 504.
Insignia seen on the battalion's vehicles,
Tunisia, 1943.

Insignia of Panzer-Abteilung
(Funklenk) 301.

Schwere Panzer-Abteilung 505.
Insignia used by the battalion from
its creation to the end of the war
(*see photo pp. 80–81*).

Schwere Panzer-Abteilung 505.
Unconfirmed variant insignia.

was the only one to use two different signs: a tiger sitting on a large
letter "W" and holding a red shield inscribed with a white cross, and a
white cross on a red shield inside a red circle. In the 507th insignia a
smith works on a sword on his anvil; the 508th has the bull motif but
on a white shield superimposed on top of a map of Italy; the 509th has
a tiger's head but this time facing right; the 510th has a dancing bear on
a black and white shield; and finally Pz-Abt (Fkl) 301 has the tank
rhombus with a second smaller black rhombus inside, perhaps to
denote the demolition vehicle (inside) with the radio-controlling tank
outside.

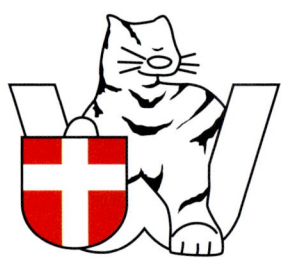

Schwere Panzer-Abteilung 506.
Insignia used in September 1943 in the
Zaporozhye area

Schwere Panzer-Abteilung 506.
Insignia thought to have been used after
the unit was re-formed in September
1944.

Schwere Panzer-Abteilung 507.
Insignia used by the battalion from its
creation to the end of the war.

Schwere Panzer-Abteilung 508.
Insignia used by the battalion from its
creation to the end of the war.

Schwere Panzer-Abteilung 509.
Insignia seen in the Shepetovka area
during the winter of 1943–4.

Schwere Panzer-Abteilung 510.
Unconfirmed insignia thought to have
been used in the unit's engagement
alongside 11th Panzer Division in the
Schaulen sector.

Waffen-SS and GD Division Those companies that were part of Waffen-SS Divisions and the Army *GD* division, naturally used their divisional sign (e.g. *GD* used the German steel helmet), while the three SS heavy tank battalions used the relevant SS Panzerkorps sign.

Vehicle Camouflage

When issued, tanks were normally painted with a base coat of dark yellow, while the turret numbers were usually in black or red with white edging and stretched almost the full height of the turret. Various camouflage schemes were painted on top of the base coat—such as sand-olive for those going to Tunisia, olive-green lines and/or red-brown spots for the Eastern Front and, in winter, a thick coat of lime/salt whitewash was applied—or, in an emergency, chalk or even white cloth. Detailed instructions were seldom issued, so it was left to the individual crew/unit to decide what was most suitable for the local terrain. A few tanks were also still painted dark gray which was an early war/prewar color scheme. Zimmerit, the anti-magnetic mine paste, also gray in color (although lighter than the paint) was often applied to Tigers before they left the factory, while some tanks were issued with special small rakes or rollers, so that the Zimmerit could be "textured" to make it more effective in repelling sticky/magnetic anti-tank charges. When the situation demanded it, foliage and branches from local trees might be used, while camouflage netting was sometimes wound around gun barrels into which small cut pieces of foliage could then be inserted—well worth the effort as the long barrel of the 8.8-cm main gun was extremely difficult to hide. As the Germans went on to the defensive much more use was made of foliage to help vehicles "hide" from possible air strikes—fine in the wooded areas of north-west Europe, but of little use in the flat plains and open steppes of Russia. In north-west Europe they also constructed thousands of camouflaged roadside shelters, for vehicles to hide in—always provided they had sufficient warning to be able to reach one undetected.

Complicated camouflage patterns were necessary in the spring, summer and fall, but plain white (paint, whitewash, etc.) liberally applied by the crew was ideal for the long, snowy winters on the Eastern Front. *(BA 458/76/37)*

Self-Help As the photographs show, the painting was done by the crew, so there was inevitably no standard pattern except in a few cases when orders to apply one had been issued by a local commander. The crew also had to use whatever means they had at their disposal to apply the paint—this might vary from sophisticated spray guns (normally worked off an engine-driven compressor), to paintbrushes, sponges, brooms, rags, etc., in other words whatever came to hand. As the war progressed and suitable paint supplies became more and more difficult to obtain, then, as Bruce Culver and Bill Murphy say in their *Panzer Colors*: ". . . the paint system was marked by a *lack* of system, and many

Taken during a moment of relaxation in Russia in 1942, these three "show off" various layers of uniform—underwear, shirt, and tunic—on the side trackguard of their Tiger. If the date is correct then they must have been members of one of the very first Tiger crews to see action in Russia. *(BA 455/20/18)*

variations in colors, patterns and application were found." As these meager supplies got even less and less, some units gave up using camouflage paint completely, so some German vehicles were just dark yellow all over (the basic color they had been when leaving the factory), while even in the snowy Ardennes, not all used white paint/whitewash. Some units, in particular from the Waffen-SS, preferred to continue to employ their standard unit camouflage painting as they had done in the past and this continued to be the case, for example, with the Tiger IIs in Budapest.

Uniforms

As the photographs show, Army tank crews wore a wide mixture of different headgear, although the black sidecap was probably the most common, while the prewar black double beret (*Schutzmütze*) had been completely abandoned in Tiger units. Most crewmen would wear the standard black Panzer uniform over a gray shirt and black tie, while adding some type of topcoat/greatcoat in winter. For working dress a variety of denim-type coveralls (one-piece or two-piece) were worn, while crewmen in Tunisia wore various combinations of tropical/shirt-sleeve order. In the depths of the Soviet winter, some crews wore white

The best way of applying camouflage paint was via a paint spray, run off the engine. Here a crew of s.Pz-Abt 503, apply the paint to their Königstiger in France in early June 1944, just prior to the Allied invasion. *(BA 321/398/91A)*

coveralls (*Schnee-Tarnung Uberzug*) as the photographs show. These snow coveralls—single piece or double—were all well-made garments with reinforced seams, buttons/button holes, drawstrings and strengthened flaps Where possible, except on coveralls, badges of rank, gallantry decorations, and other insignia were worn on all types of uniforms, including some cuff titles. Knight's Crosses were always worn at the throat, with the ribbon underneath the shirt collar.

The Waffen-SS tank crews also wore the same black uniform as those in the Army, although in the mid-war years a slightly modified version was produced for the SS (front closure was vertical instead of slanting, lapels were smaller). A one-piece combat coverall in special "SS pattern" camouflage cloth was produced in 1943, then the following year, a two-piece uniform—also in camouflage cloth—that was cut on similar lines to the black Panzer uniform and was widely worn in 1944–5, together with a camouflaged version of the field cap. An oddity was a consignment of submariners' leather coats and pants that had been ordered from Italy but passed on to the SS when not required because of the scaled down U-boat activity. They were not much liked due to their heavy weight that made them very tiring to wear.

Tanks

The first 50 Tiger IIs built had the more streamlined Porsche turret, which had an obvious shot trap below the turret mounting, while the rest had the simpler Henschel turret without electric drive, which had made the Porsche turrets so expensive. While Tiger I was in service with all of the heavy tank battalions, Tiger II only replaced it fully or partially in certain battalions:

s.Pz-Abt 501: completely re-equipped in July 1944

s.Pz-Abt 503: only partially re-equipped (one company) in June 1944; the other two received Tiger Is. This was the first unit to receive Tiger IIs, apart from the Training Battalion (500) and the Waffenamt. After taking casualties in the west it would be fully re-equipped in September 1944

Specifications

	Tiger I (PzKpfw VI Ausf E)	*Tiger II (PzKpfw VI Ausf B)*
Entered service:	1942	1944
Crew:	5	5
Weight:	56 tons	68 tons
Dimensions		
Length:	27 ft 8.5 in	33 ft 9 in
Height:	9f t 10 in	10 ft 1 in
Width:	11 ft 8 in	11 ft 10.7 in
Armament		
Main:	8.8-cm KwK 36 L/56	8.8-cm KwK 43 L/71
Muzzle velocity:	2,657 ft/sec	3,340 ft/sec
Rounds carried:	92	84 (68 stowed)
Secondary:	2 x 7.92mm MG	3 x 7.92mm MG
	(one coaxial, one in hull)	(one coaxial, one in hull, one AA)
Armor (max):	100 mm	150 mm
Powerplant:	Maybach HL 210P45 V12 gasoline	Maybach HL 230P30 V12 gasoline
Speed:	22.9 mph	21.75 mph
Range:	121 miles	105 miles
Numbers built:	1,355 (Jul 1942–Aug 1944)	489 (Jan 1944–Mar 1945)

s.Pz-Abt 505: completely re-equipped in September 1944

s.Pz-Abt 506: completely re-equipped in August 1944

s.Pz-Abt 507: only partially re-equipped in March 1945, the rest receiving Tiger I

s.Pz-Abt 509: completely re-equipped September 1944

SS s.Pz-Abt 101 (501): completely re-equipped

SS s.Pz-Abt 502: partly re-equipped February/March 1945

SS s.Pz-Abt 503: partly re-equipped January 1945

      (*Source:* Gudgin: *The Tiger Tanks*)

Tiger I & II Gun Performance		
PzGr 40 and PzGr 40/43 respectively Penetration in mm at ranges shown		
	KwK 36	*KwK 43*
500 m	155	217
1,000 m	138	197
2,000 m	110	152

PzKpfw III

Often described as being the backbone of the German Panzer divisions were their medium (15–25-ton) tanks, the PzKpfw III and IV, of which the PzKpfw III, Ausf L/M/N were typical of those serving in Tiger units. A variety of different models were used in the heavy tank battalions. However, ideally those in the heavy tank companies were the earlier models that mounted the 5-cm gun, while those in the separate light tank platoon were the more modern N model, which mounted a 7.5-cm L/24 gun which had a much better armor-piercing capability and a more effective HE round as well.

Their basic job in the heavy tank companies was to provide close support to the Tigers, but after their place as gun tanks had been taken

The other gun tank found in the heavy tank battalions was the PzKpfw III, in various marks mainly either the Ausf K/L/M and/or the Ausf N. The former were armed with various models of the 5-cm gun, but the latter mounted the short-barrelled, more powerful 7.5-cm gun, which had a better armor-penetrating round as well as more effective high explosive ammunition. The PzKpfw IIIs were there to provide the Tigers with close-in fire support against enemy infantry. (*Tank Museum 3348/D5*)

18 Tiger Is (Ausf E) were converted into the 65-ton 38-cm Tiger-Mörser, which fired a massive rocket-assisted shell. *(Compendium)*

Most of the Tiger (P) production was diverted to to be used for the heavy tank destroyer Elefant (also called Ferdinand after its designer). Some 90 were produced and they were first used in the Kursk offensive. Here senior Russian officers inspect a captured Elefant. General Rokossovsky is second on the right on the ground, while General Telegin is leaning on the barrel of the tank destroyer's deadly 8.8-cm gun. Note the strikes on the front of the turret. *(Author's Collection)*

by additional Tigers, they were also sometimes de-turreted and used as replenishment vehicles. One battalion (the 505th), it is said, also used its obsolescent PzKpfw IIIs to carry bridging materials and suchlike, having also first removed their turrets. In addition there is evidence that PzKpfw IV gun tanks were sometimes to be found in some of the heavy tank battalions, being used in the same manner as the PzKpfw IIIs.

Tiger Variants

While these variants were never a part of the heavy tank battalions, the Tiger chassis was used for three important types—two were superheavy tank destroyers, one whose name was most appropriately Elefant and the other Jagdtiger, the latter being the heaviest AFV to see action during World War II. The third was a somewhat bizarre assault rocket mortar.

Elefant Sturmgeschütz mit 8.8-cm PaK 43/2. Based on Tiger (P) and also called Ferdinand, this heavy tank destroyer weighed over 65 tons and mounted the long version of the 8.8-cm gun. First saw action at Kursk. 90 produced.

Jagdtiger A heavy tank destroyer, which at 70 tons was the heaviest tank/tank destroyer to see action during the war. It mounted a 12.8-cm PaK 44 L/55 main gun that dealt easily with any Allied AFV. It was issued to only two combat units and saw service in the Battle of the Bulge and in the defense of the Fatherland. 77 only produced.

Sturmtiger 38-cm RW61 auf Sturmmörser Tiger—a 65-ton assault rocket mortar based on the Tiger I chassis. Designed for demolishing enemy strongpoints, it was used mainly in the defense of the German homeland. 18 only converted.

The massive Jagdtiger at the U.K. Tank Museum. *(Tank Museum 5547/A5)*

The largest and heaviest AFV to see action in WWII was the enormous Jagdtiger, whose 12.8-cm gun could deal with anything the Allies could produce. Here two GIs inspect an abandoned Jagdtiger.
(Tank Museum 14/4)

Other Vehicles

In addition to its tanks every heavy tank battalion had a number of other vehicles, some armored, others soft-skinned. Numbers naturally varied with casualties, but all played their own special and important role. For example there were:

Tracked demolition charge layers. As has been explained, one unit (Panzer-Abteilung [Funklenk] 301), and one subunit (Panzer-Kompanie [Funklenk] 316) both had a number of tracked demolition charge vehicles (Borgward IV Ladungsträger) that were controlled by radio from Tiger tanks. The charge-layer vehicle had a single crewman who drove the vehicle while it was out of action, but it could then be radio-controlled to its target (a pillbox or other fortification), the charge would be deposited, the charge carrier moved out of harm's way, and the charge exploded. The B IV was used successfully to help clear Russian minefields during Operation Zitadelle at Kursk.

Recovery/mechanics' vehicles. Vehicles used by the mechanics included: the Bergepanther—an armored recovery vehicle based on the Panther chassis; 18-ton Zugkraftwagen—heavy prime movers (two or three of which were needed to tow a single Tiger); Kran Kraftfahrzeug—prime mover with 10-tonne portable gantry crane.

FlaKPanzers. Two types of FlaKPanzer were built using the

PzKpfw IV chassis: Wirbelwind, a quad 2-cm mount (Flakvierling 38) and Ostwind, a single 3.7-cm FlaK 43/1 L/60. The latter began to replace the former from August 1944. Both would have been replaced by Kugelblitz (a light anti-aircraft tank mounting the 2-cm MK 103/38) but only two were ever built. The 2-cm Flakvierling 38 auf Fahrgestell Zugkraftwagen 8t (Sd Kfz 7/1) was the halftrack vehicle. Battalions held up to four of each AA tank version and/or up to six of the halftrack version, the former replacing the latter as the war progressed (see table).

Halftracks. Battalions held a mixture of halftracks used for a variety of tasks such as command and signal, reconnaissance, weapons and personnel carrying, ranging from 1-ton up to 8-ton versions and including the little Kettenkrad tracked two-man vehicle for reconnaissance missions. As the photographs show, the battalions also employed light, medium, and heavy halftracks in these roles.

Soft-skinned vehicles. A range of staff cars and trucks were held, mostly capable of cross-country movement (although not all), some being of civilian origin,

Motorcycles. Motorcycles of various types with and without sidecars were widely used for scouting and reconnaissance duties as well as message carrying.

A Tiger belonging to s.Pz-Abt 505 passing two of the battalion's light flak halftracks—the 2-cm Flakvierling 38 Sd Kfz 7/1. *(BA 90/3947/12)*

ABOVE: The Kettenkrad. This strange little vehicle was the NSU HK 101 tracked motor-cycle Sd Kfz 2, used mainly for reconnaissance missions by the heavy tank battalions. Some 8,345 of these vehicles were produced, using a 4-cylinder 36-hp Opel Olympia engine, driving front sprockets via a 3-speed transmission and 2-speed auxiliary box. *(Tank Museum 2908/F1)*

RIGHT: The Borgward B IV demolition-charge layer. This 3.6-ton vehicle was designed to carry a charge to a specific target. The charge was then dropped, the vehicle backed away, and the charge was set off, remotely by radio, from a control vehicle—in this case a Tiger tank. *(Tank Museum 7290/A2)*

Bergepanther. While only six Tigers (3 x Tiger (P) chassis and 3 x Tiger Ausf E) were ever converted to recovery vehicles, some 355 Bergepanther were produced (240 Ausf A and 107 Ausf G). Eight Ausf A were converted from gun-tank Panthers, the rest being purpose-built between June 1943 and the end of the war. Bergepanthers were used by the workshop companies of the heavy tank battalions to replace the Sd Kfz 9 heavy tractors. *(Tank Museum 4840/A2)*

German equivalent of the Allied amphibious Jeep was this VW 166 K2 Schwimmwagen being used here for route control by I SS Panzerkorps *Leibstandarte* in northern France in the summer of 1944. It is guiding SS-Haupsturmführer Möbius (in turret) while the rest of the crew are on *Jabo* watch. The *Schwimmer* had a hinged three-bladed propeller giving it a water speed of 6 mph. *(BA 299/1804/5)*

ABOVE, BOTH: Later in the war large commercial trailers were sometimes used to carry Tiger I and II. This photo shows a Tiger 1 being transported on a Gotha 80-ton tank transporter trailer just after the end of the war, when it was bound for England. *(Barry Hook)*

All the heavy tank battalions' support vehicles were motorized, whether wheeled or tracked, but of course that was not the case in the rest of the German Army which still had thousands of horses pulling a variety of carts/trailers/sledges.

Given below is a list of the numbers of these vehicles in the heavy tank battalions.

Heavy Tank Battalion Support Vehicles

Vehicle Type	July 1st, 1943	Jan 1st, 1945	Remarks
FlakPanzer	0	8	(4 x 3.7-cm + 4 x Quad 2-cm)
8-ton 4 x 2-cm FlaK	6	3	AA on halftrack
SchützenPanzer	10	11	Halftrack
Bergepanther	0	5	Armored recovery vehicle (based on Panther)
18-ton Zugkraftwagen	8	7	18-ton recovery halftrack
1-ton Zugkraftwagen	8	13	1-ton halftrack
Kettenkrad	0	14	halftrack motorcycle
Beiwagenkrad	25	0	motorcycle + sidecar
Solokrad	17	6	motorcycle
Personenkraftwagen (geländegänig)	64	38	cross-country staff car
Personenkraftwagen zivil	2	1	truck (limited cross-country)
Lastkraftwagen (geländegänig)	111	84	cross-country truck
Lastkraftwagen zivil	24	34	truck (limited cross-country)
Maultier	0	6	truck converted to halftrack
Kran-Kraftfahrzeug[1]	3	3	10-ton portable crane
Totals	278	323	

Note: Some sources say just one crane per battalion not three.

Source: Schneider, Tigers in Combat

LEFT: Additional flak protection for the heavy tank battalions was provided by Wirbelwind, a 2-cm Flakvierling mounted on an obsolete PzKpfw IV chassis. Fewer than 90 were produced, some replacing the Sd Kfz 7/1. *(Compendium)*

LEFT: Both sides made use of captured equipment. Here an Allied half track captured in Tunisia draws a trailer containing precious spare Tiger roadwheels. *(BA 557/1018/28A)*

BELOW: A heavy 4 x 4 universal cross-country car passes a Tiger "somewhere in Tunisia" in 1943. There were both open (as here) and closed versions of this car. *(BA 557/1018/26A)*

PERSONALITIES

An orders group of tank commanders of SS s.Pz-Abt 101 during training in the Beauvais sector of north-east Normandy before joining the Normandy front. The battalion commander, SS-Sturmbannführer Hein von Westernhagen, is standing facing the camera wearing the camouflaged tunic (1943 model) and a 1940 pattern officer's black cap with aluminum piping. Hanno Rasch, on his left, the commander of Tiger 311, is wearing the gray/green motorcycle raincoat. *(BA 299/1805/3)*

Pen Pictures

There is room in this book for only a small cross-section of examples from the large number of notable unit commanders, Knight's Cross winners, and tank aces who served with the heavy tank battalions, so I have chosen just four: Franz Bäke, who had the signal honor of commanding the most unusual heavy tank unit in the *Panzerwaffe*; Helmut Hudel, who commanded Heavy Tank Battalion 508, Otto Carius, famous tank ace of Heavy Tank Battalion 202, and finally, Michael Wittmann another tank ace who was in SS Heavy Tank Battalion 101.

Generalmajor Dr (med. dent.) Franz Bäke, was born in Schwarzenfels in February 1898. He volunteered in 1915 and ended the Great War as an artillery officer cadet. Between the wars he studied dentistry, graduating in 1923. Mobilized in 1939, he served with various armored units rising quickly through the ranks to Oberst in May 1944. He was promoted to Generalmajor in April 1945. A much decorated tank commander, he also took part in the largest-ever tank battle at Kursk in July 1943. His Panzer battalion was part of III Panzer Corps' assault from Belgorod on the south of Kursk salient and the highlight was Bäke's infiltration into the Soviet defenses under cover of night in which he used a captured T-34 commanded by a fluent Russian speaker to lead his force. He had also given orders to the Panzergrenadiers riding on the tanks to smoke and act casually. In this way they penetrated as far as the outskirts of Rzhavets before being discovered and knocked out some 72 Russian tanks for the loss of just four Tigers. Later Bäke recalled:

Oberstleutnant Dr Franz Bäke commanded a unique force including a heavy tank battalion and inflicted considerable losses on the enemy for which he was awarded the Knight's Cross, then the Oak Leaves. *(Bundesarchiv)*

> After about six miles our T-34 went on strike. Moved no doubt by national sentiment, it stopped and blocked the road. So our men had to climb out of their tanks and, in spite of the Russians standing all around them watching curiously, they had to haul the T-34 off the road and push it into a ditch in order to clear the way for the rest of the formation. In spite of the order that not a word of German was to be spoken, a few German curses were heard. Never before had I winced so much because of a curse as at Rzhavets. But the Russians still did not notice anything. The crew of our T-34 was picked up and on we moved. (Quoted in Robin Cross, *Citadel*)

Already the holder of the Knight's Cross (awarded on January 11th, 1943), he received his Oak Leaves (262nd to be awarded, on August 1st, 1943) for this operation and others during Zitadelle.

On the next noteworthy occasion Bäke's command comprised s.Pz-Abt 503 (with 35 Tiger Is), 2nd Battalion, Panzer Regiment 23 (47 Panthers), a self-propelled artillery battalion and an engineer battalion that had had to develop specialist bridging skills to be able to assist his two battalions of such heavy tanks. This combat group was formed in January 1944 and its first task was to deal with a thrust toward Vinnitsa by a massive Soviet force of some five tank corps. The action began on the evening of the 26th and lasted for the next five days and nights. During the fighting, Bäke's group destroyed some 267 tanks and 156 guns of various types in the area Oratov–Balabanovka. His losses were just one Tiger and four Panthers. Higher commanders were so surprised that they at first doubted his figures and demanded clarification. He was awarded his Swords for this action. Heavy Panzer Regiment *Bäke* went on to provide the cutting edge for III Panzer Corps

Battalion Commanders

s.Pz-Abt 501

Major Hans-Georg Lueder	May 42–Feb 43
Major Erich Löwe	Sep–Dec 43 (MIA 23 Dec)
Oberstleutnant von Legat	Jan–Aug 44
Major Saemisch	Aug 44–Jan 45
	(KIA 13 Jan)

s.Pz-Abt 502

Major Richard Märker	Aug–Nov 42
Hauptmann Wollschläger	Nov 42–Feb 43
Major Richter	Feb–Jul 43
Hauptmann Schmidt	Jul–Aug 43
Hauptmann Lange	Aug–Oct 43
Major Willy Jähde	Oct 43–Mar 44
Major Schwaner	Apr–Aug 44
Hauptmann von Foerster	Aug 44–Apr 45

s.Pz-Abt 503

Oberstleutnant Post	May 42–Jan 43
Oberstleutnant Hoheisel	Jan–May 43
Hauptmann Graf Kageneck	May 43–Feb 44
Hauptmann Fromme	Feb–Dec 44
Hauptmann Dr N. von Diest-Koerber	
	Dec 44–May 45

s.Pz-Abt 504

Major August Seidensticker	Feb–May 43
Hauptmann Kühn	Nov 43–May 45
Major Nill	Sep 44–May 45

s.Pz-Abt 505

Major Bernhard Sauvant	Feb–Aug 43
Hauptmann von Carlowitz	Aug–Sep 43 (KIA 15 Sep)
Hauptmann Werner Freiherr von Beschwitz	
	Sep 43–Nov 44
Major Senfft von Pilsach	Nov 44–Apr 45

s.Pz-Abt 506

Major Gerhard Willing	Jul–Oct 43 (KIA 23 Oct)
Major Lange	Nov 43–Jan 45
Hauptmann Heiligenstadt	Jan–Feb 45
	(captured 9 Feb)
Major von Römer	Feb–Apr 45

s.Pz-Abt 507

Major Erich Schmidt	Sep 43–Aug 44
Hauptmann Fritz Schröck	Aug 44–May 45

s.Pz-Abt 508

Major Helmut Hudel	Jan–May 44
Hauptmann Selter	Aug 44–May 45

s.Pz-Abt 509

Hauptmann von Lüttich	Aug–Nov 43
Major Gierka	Nov 43–Feb 44
Hauptmann Radke	Feb–Mar 44 (KIA 4 Mar)

s.Pz-Abt 510

Major Kurt Gilbert	Jun 44–May 45

s.Pz-Abt (Fl) 301

Hauptmann Kramer	Sep 42–Apr 45

III./Pz-Regt *GD*

Major Gomille	Jun 43–Apr 44
Oberstleutnant Baumungk	Apr–Aug 44 (WIA 9 Aug)
Hauptmann Bock	Aug 44–Apr 45

SS s.Pz-Abt 101 (SS s.Pz-Abt 501)

SS-Sturmbannführer Hein von Westernhagen	
	Jul–Nov 43
SS-Obersturmbannführer Leiner	
	Nov 43–Feb 44
SS-Obersturmbannführer Hein von Westernhagen	
	Feb 44–Mar 45
SS-Sturmbannführer Kling	Mar–May 45

SS s.Pz-Abt 102 (SS s.Pz-Abt 502)

SS-Sturmbannführer Lackmann	
	Jan–Mar 44
SS-Sturmbannführer Weiss	Mar–Aug 44
SS-Sturmbannführer Kurt Hartrampf	
	Aug 44–May 45

SS s.Pz-Abt 103 (SS s.Pz-Abt 503)

SS-Sturmbannführer Paetsch	Jul 43–Feb 44
SS-Obersturmbannführer Leiner	
	Feb 44–Jan 45
SS-Sturmbannführer Friedrich Herzig	
	Jan 45–May 45

Source: Schneider, *Tigers in Combat*

as it went to the relief of another German force in the area. When s.Pz-Abt 503 was withdrawn that spring to be converted to Tiger II, its place was taken by s.Pz-Abt 509. Bäke was taken prisoner on May 8th, 1945, released early in 1947, and died at Hagen in Westphalia on December 12th, 1978.

Major Helmut Hudel was born in Raunheim in July 1915 and at the age of nineteen he volunteered for the Army and was commissioned in 1936. After a period on attachment to the Kriegsschule in Potsdam, he joined Panzer Regiment 7 while it was part of 10th Panzer Division and was soon fighting his first battles around Minsk and Smolensk. Promoted to Hauptmann in March 1942, Hudel was decorated with the Knight's Cross on May 27th, 1942, while he was serving with a battlegroup of 20th Panzer Division around Vyazma. Later in 1942, his division was sent to Tunisia, to help counter the Allied landings there. Hudel was awarded the Oak Leaves to his Knight's Cross on April 2nd, 1943, in recognition of his skill and bravery while commanding the 1st Battalion of Panzer Regiment 7.

Major Helmut Hudel. *(Bundesarchiv)*

He was transferred from North Africa before the Axis surrender there and, in January 1944, was given command of Heavy Tank Battalion 508 that was sent to Italy shortly afterward to help contain the Allied beachhead at Anzio. In May 1944 he was off again to command the reserve Panzer training battalion of the elite *Grossdeutschland* Panzer Division. He stayed with this unit until February 1945, when he was given command of the Panzer Lehr Regiment, which was sent to Holland and later to attack the U.S. bridgehead at Remagen. The regiment was decimated in this and subsequent actions and finished the war with just fifteen tanks. Hudel died in 1985, aged 69

Oberleutnant Otto Carius Born in Zweibrücken in May 1922, Carius joined the Army in 1940 and became a tank crewman in one of the Czech-built PzKpfw 38(t) that had been "acquired" by the *Panzerwaffe*. His first action was in the German assault on the Soviet Union in June 1941 and he went on fighting on the Central Front for about a year, when he was selected to attend officer training and was subsequently commissioned into the Panzer branch and posted to s.Pz-Abt 502. He rapidly earned a considerable reputation for his success in knocking out enemy tanks in a number of amazing tank duels. He was awarded the Knight's Cross in May 1944 and the Oak Leaves in July the same year. The following month he was posted to the armor center at Paderborn and took command of a company in the recently formed Heavy Tank Destroyer Battalion 512, equipped with the massive Jagdtiger. He fought in the series of defensive battles along the Rhine in March and April 1945, before surrendering to the Americans. During his five years

Knight's Cross Winners
(Awarded while serving with Heavy Tank Battalions)

	date of award	remarks
Beschwitz, Major Werner Freiherr von	27 Jul 44	CO s.Pz-Abt 505
Bleyer, Feldwebel Werner	24 Feb 45	Posthumous
Bölter, Leutnant Johannes	16 Apr 44	Oak Leaves 10 Sep 44
Bromann, SS-Untersturmbannführer Karl	29 Apr 45	
Burmester, Hauptmann Hans-Jürgen	02 Sep 44	
Carius, Leutnant Otto	04 May 44	Oak Leaves 27 Jul 44
Carpaneto, Unteroffizier Alfredo	28 Mar 45	Posthumous
Diest-Koerber, Hauptmann Dr N. von	01 May 45	CO s.Pz-Abt 503
Egger, SS-Oberscharführer Paul	28 Apr 45	
Ernst, Hauptmann Albert	22 Jan 44	
Fey, SS-Oberscharführer Will	29 Apr 45	
Gebhardt, Feldwebel Rolf	30 Sep 44	
Gilbert, Major Kurt	07 Apr 45	CO s.Pz-Abt 510
Hartrampf, SS-Sturmbannführer Kurt	28 Apr 45	CO SS s.Pz-Abt 502
Heinrich, Leutnant Willi	09 Dec 44	
Herzig, SS-Sturmbannführer Friedrich	29 Apr 45	CO SS s.Pz-Abt 503
Hoehne, Leutnant Helmut	09 Dec 44	
Jähde, Major Willy	16 Mar 44	CO s.Pz-Abt 502
Kageneck, Hauptmann Clemens Graf	04 Aug 43	Oak Leaves 26 Jun 44
Kalls, SS-Obersturmführer Alois	28 Aug 44	
Kannenberg, Stabsfeldwebel Kurt	09 Dec 44	Posthumous
Kerscher, Feldwebel Albert	23 Oct 44	
Kling, SS-Hauptsturmführer Heinrich	23 Feb 44	
Knauth, Oberleutnant Dr Wilhelm	14 Nov 43	
Körner, Leutnant Helmut	03 Dec 43	
Körner SS-Hauptscharführer Karl	29 Apr 45	
Koltermann, Oberleutnant Wolfgang	11 Mar 45	
Kramer, Unteroffizier Heinz	06 Oct 44	MIA Jan 45

Tiger's Place in History

"As an object of popular enthusiasm the tank stands in line a long way behind many other evocative machines. For all that, some famous tanks have impressed themselves on the general public to the extent that they have become household names and, among these, the German heavy tank Tiger is probably best known of all."

From: Introduction, *Tiger! The Tiger Tank a British View*, ed. David Fletcher

of tank service he had been awarded the Panzer Badge in Silver for over 100 combat engagements, the Iron Cross 1st and 2nd Class, as well as his Knight's Cross with Oak Leaves. A fearless tank ace, he was credited with knocking out some 150 enemy tanks. Postwar, he went back to his peacetime occupation as a pharmacist.

SS-Hauptsturmführer Michael Wittmann was born in Vogelthal, Oberpfalz, in April 1914. A farmer's son, he worked on the farm until he joined the Army (Infantry Regiment 19) in 1934. Nearly three years later, he joined the Waffen-SS—the *Leibstandarte Adolf Hitler* Division at Lichterfelde Barracks in Berlin. By the time war began he was an

	date of award	remarks
Litzke, Oberfeldwebel Erich	20 Oct 44	
Löwe, Major Erich	04 Sep 40	Oak Leaves 24 Dec 43
		(when CO s.Pz-Abt 501)
Müller, Feldwebel Johann	23 Oct 44	
Rampell, Oberfeldwebel Josef	14 Dec 43	
Ratajczak, Oberfeldwebel Edmund	10 Feb 45	
Rinke, Oberleutnant Adolf	17 Apr 45	Posthumous
Röhrig, Oberfähnrich Oskar	04 Jul 44	
Sauvant, Major Bernhard	30 Nov 42	Oak Leaves 28 Jul 43
		(when CO s.Pz-Abt 505)
Schäfer, SS-Untersturmbannführer Oskar	29 Apr 45	
Scherf, Oberleutnant Walter	23 Feb 44	
Schnepf, Leutnant Wilhelm	31 Jan 45	Posthumous
Schmidt, Major Erich	09 Jun 44	CO s.Pz-Abt 507
		(Oak Leaves 9 May 45)
Schröck, Hauptmann Fritz	05 Sep 44	CO s.Pz-Abt 507
Seidensticker, Major August	18 Nov 43	CO s.Pz-Abt 504
Speckter, Oberleutnant Hans	09 Apr 44	
Staudegger, SS-Unterscharführer Franz	10 Jul 43	
Terriete, Leutnant Heinrich	22 Jul 43	
Tischendorf, Hauptmann Herbert	11 Mar 05	
Wendorf, SS-Untersturmführer Helmut	12 Feb 44	
Woll, SS-Rottenführer Balthasar	16 Jan 44	
Willing, Major Gerhard	29 Oct 43	CO s.Pz-Abt 506
Wirsching, Oberleutnant Maximilian	07 Feb 45	
Wittmann, SS-Untersturmführer Michael	14 Jan 44	Oak Leaves 30 Jan 44,
		Swords 22 Jun 44

Source: Walther-Peer Fellgiebel, *Elite of the Third Reich*

Tiger Aces

(enemy tanks destroyed):

Feldwebel Knispel	162
Oberleutnant Carius	150
Hauptmann Bölter	144
SS-Hauptsturmführer Wittmann[1]	121
SS-Oberscharführer Egger	113
Oberfähnrich Rondorf	106
SS-Oberscharführer Körner	over 100
Feldwebel Gärtner	over 100
Feldwebel Kerscher	100
SS-Obersturmführer Wendorf	95
Oberfeldwebel Litzke	76
Oberleutnant Knauth	68
SS-Untersturmführer Bromann	66
SS-Oberscharführer Brandt	57
SS-Unterscharführer Warmbrunn	57
Oberfeldwebel Mausberg	over 50
SS-Sturmbannführer Kling	51
Unteroffizier Kramer	50
Feldwebel Carpeneto	50
Feldwebel Müller	50

Note: Other sources credit Wittmann with 138 tanks (and 132 AT guns).

Source: Schneider, *Tigers in Combat*

Unterscharführer (corporal), and he took part in the *Blitzkrieg* on Poland in command of an armored car. Next, in the campaign in the Balkans, he was in command of an assault gun. From the Balkans the *Leibstandarte* thrust into Russia, where his coolness under fire soon earned him an Iron Cross 2nd Class, then a few months later he was awarded the Iron Cross, 1st Class, plus the Panzer Assault and Wound Badges. He came to prominence when he personally knocked out six enemy tanks after being attacked by eight. His leadership potential was quickly appreciated and he was sent away to officers' school at Bad Tölz, to be commissioned in the rank of Untersturmführer (2nd lieutenant) in December 1942. Early in January 1943, he took over a Tiger tank

Oberleutnant Dr Wilhelm Knauth receiving his Knight's Cross on November 17th, 1944. He was the company commander of 3. Kompanie, s.Pz-Abt 505 and had been awarded his medal on November 14th, 1943. *(BA 278/873/5)*

and his phenomenal career as a tank ace began. By the time he was awarded the Knight's Cross (January 14th, 1944) he had knocked out 66 Soviet tanks. Just a week later when he was promoted to SS-Obersturmführer (lieutenant) his tank kills had almost doubled to 117! His Oak Leaves followed swiftly and in April 1944 he was promoted to command a company of SS s.Pz-Abt 101. His undoubted skill and courage were cleverly manipulated by the Nazi propaganda machine, so he had become a household name even before his incredible feat at Villers-Bocage, where, virtually on his own, he annihilated the entire advance guard of the leading battle group of 7th Armoured Division, for which he was awarded his Swords (71st holder of this award)—just five months since the original award of his Knight's Cross.

He was then offered a safe training job, but refused to leave his Tiger company, and he was killed on August 8th, 1944, when his Tiger I and others were knocked out by several Sherman Fireflies of the Northamptonshire Yeomanry. At that time he had been credited by some sources with the destruction of a staggering 138 Allied tanks and assault guns and 132 anti-tank guns, in less than two years. Described as being an earnest, quiet and thoughtful man, who was highly admired

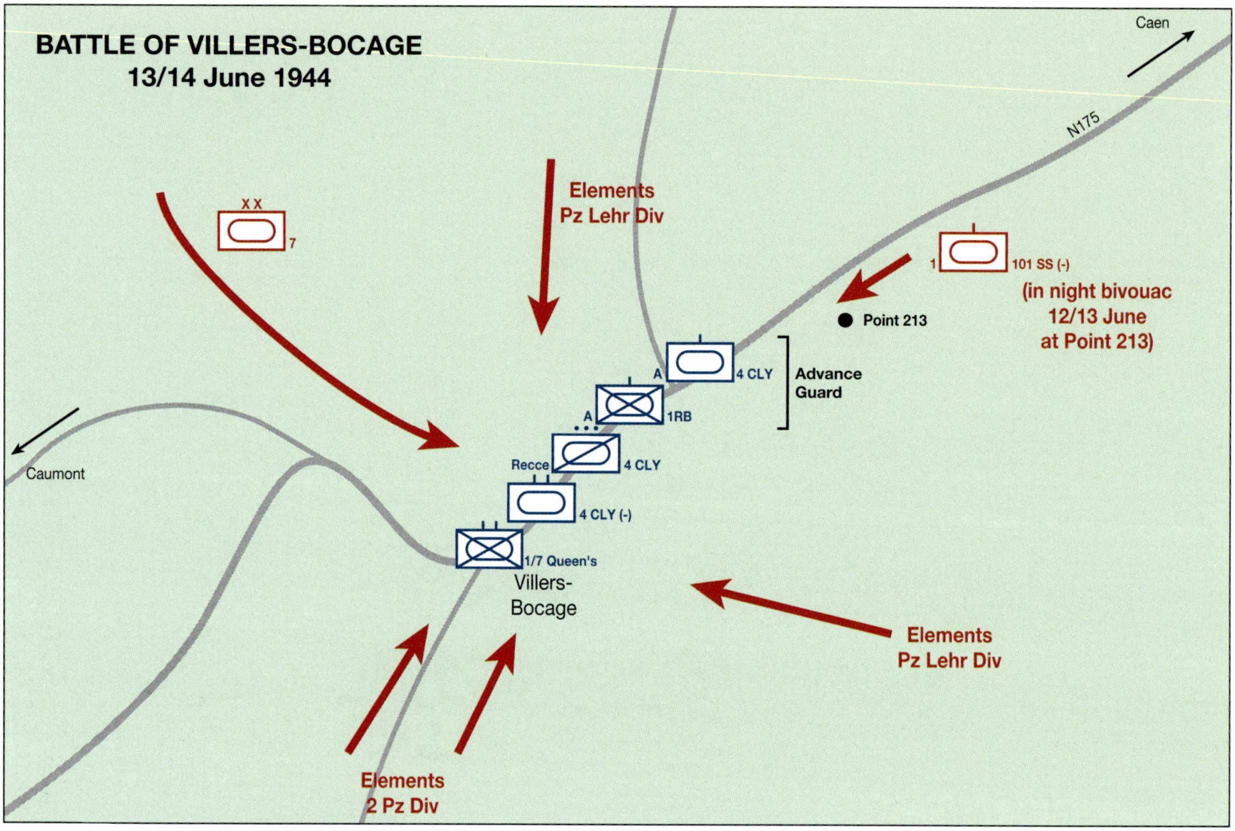

BATTLE OF VILLERS-BOCAGE
13/14 June 1944

Caen

N175

Elements
Pz Lehr Div

XX
7

1 | 101 SS (-)

● Point 213

(in night bivouac
12/13 June
at Point 213)

A | 4 CLY | Advance
Guard

A | 1RB

Caumont

Recce | 4 CLY

4 CLY (-)

1/7 Queen's

Villers-
Bocage

Elements
Pz Lehr Div

Elements
2 Pz Div

by both his comrades and his senior officers, he was one of the most successful tank aces ever and undoubtedly deserves his place in the annals of military history. Kurt "Panzer" Meyer, who was the youngest divisional commander (1st SS Panzer Division) in the Waffen-SS, spoke of Wittmann as: ". . . dying as he had lived—brave and dashing, a living example to his tank crews."

SS-Obersturmführer Michael Wittmann was already an acknowledged tank ace with hundreds of tanks and anti-tank guns to his credit well before his remarkable action at Villers-Bocage for which he was promoted to SS-Hauptsturmführer and awarded the coveted Swords to his Knight's Cross (he already held the Oak Leaves). *(BA 299/1802/8)*

ASSESSMENT

Basic Characteristics

All tanks, especially heavy tanks like Tiger, are a careful blend of those three most important basic characteristics of any tank: firepower, protection, and mobility. Firepower was naturally the most important as it was the *raison d'être* for the Tiger, namely to kill enemy tanks. However, mobility and protection were also very significant so that Tiger could carry its firepower about from location to location on the battlefield, with its crew and weapon system properly protected from enemy fire. Therefore, while there is no argument that firepower must take priority, protection can be achieved both from thick armor and/or from mobility, allowing the tank to move swiftly from cover to cover and not to be hindered by obstacles, continuous breakdowns, etc. Thus,

The group of light staff cars behind the Tiger include a light car 4 x 2, universally known as the Kübelwagen (head-on), and a 4 x 4 Volkswagen 87. *(BA 458/77/12)*

getting the right balance between protection and mobility is vital and it is true to say that, while Tiger I and Tiger II were both well protected, they were both too heavy and underpowered for their size and weight.

The Allies carried out a number of studies of Tiger and its battlefield ability both during the war and afterward. Their findings were that they considered it to be: "uncomfortable, spartan, heavy and its overall mobility performance inadequate," while the views of the German crews who fought in Tiger were quite the opposite; they considered it to be: "spacious, comfortable and, above all, safe." Better-protected crews meant longer lives and more experienced crewmen, thus more kills per tank. It is interesting to see that just counting up the claimed kills of the heavy tank battalions one reaches a figure of over 8,600 enemy tanks knocked out, plus thousands of artillery and anti-tank guns. The tank kills alone average out at over 600 per battalion. This is a large figure, but it is made all the more remarkable when one remembers that just two of the heavy tank battalions (502 and 503) were responsible for knocking out an incredible 1,400 and 1,700 enemy tanks respectively. To achieve such a kill-rate required highly trained, battle-experienced crews, who were able to live on the battlefield despite everything that was thrown against them

OPPOSITE, TOP: It took at least two (ideally three) of the 18-ton Sd Kfz 9 half tracks to tow a Tiger, as seen here on the Eastern Front during the Zitadelle offensive. Some 2,500 were built, primarily for the recovery of heavy tanks, although some were used as artillery tractors. *(BA 22/2926/11A)*

LEFT: The American T26E3 "General Pershing." (named after General "Black Jack" Pershing of Mexico and WWI fame) could also knock out a Tiger at reasonably long ranges, but of course did not enter service until the war in Europe was almost over. The first Pershings to see action did not do so until February 25th, 1945, when 3rd Armored Division was attacking across the River Roer. *(Tank Museum 3030/A6)*

Tiger Tamers

M26 Pershing Nevertheless, despite the Tiger's battlefield power, it could be and was knocked out by enemy tank guns and anti-tank guns. For example, writing in *Death Traps*, Belton Y. Cooper commented on the M26 Pershing's 90-mm T15E1 gun thus:

> The M26 was the first totally new main battle tank that we had . . . it weighed 47½ tons, and had four inches of armor at 45 degrees on the glacis plate. Its sides were two inches of armor and the turret about six inches in front, plus a five-inch mantlet . . . its wider tracks made it comparable to German tanks on soft, muddy terrain . . . Although its muzzle velocity was still less than that of a Panther or King Tiger, it was by far the best tank we had at the time . . . When we looked at the target [a knocked-out JagdPanzer IV], I was dumbfounded. The 90-mm projectile penetrated four inches of armor; went through the five-inch final drive differential shaft, the fighting compartment, and the rear partition of the fighting compartment; penetrated the four and a half inch crankshaft of the Maybach engine and the one-inch rear armor plate; and dug itself into the ground so deep that we could not locate it. Although we had been told by the Ordnance officers from Aberdeen [the U.S.

OPPOSITE, BOTTOM: Maintenance and repairs were also hard work, especially in field conditions. The mechanics of the Tiger workshop companies certainly earned their pay. *(Tank Museum 2907/A/5)*

Army Proving Ground in Maryland] that the tank gun would penetrate thirteen inches of armor at a hundred yards, it was still difficult to believe this awesome power. We all realized that we had a weapon that could blast hell out of even the most powerful German Mark VI Tiger.

And U.S. Pershing tank crews went on to prove this possible. One tank commander, Sergeant Nick Mashlonik of 3rd Armored Division told me the following story some years ago:

Our first exposure to the enemy with the new M26 was very fruitful. We were hit hard by the Germans from Elsdorf. The enemy appeared to have much armor as we received a lot of direct fire and this kept us pinned down. Our casualties kept mounting and the CO of our company asked me if I thought I could knock the Tiger out that was almost destroying us . . . The German Tiger was slightly dug in and this meant it would be more difficult to destroy, however I decided that I could take this Tiger with my 90-mm.

Mashlonik's M26 was in a defilade position, more or less hidden from the enemy by a little valley. He detailed his driver and gunner to accompany him—he would act as gunner while the gunner would load:

Even the Tiger could be destroyed from the outset of its operational service, as the remains of this duo belonging to 501. s.Pz-Abt and photographed in Tunisia show, but the Allies normally paid a heavy price for such success. *(Tank Museum 371/18)*

We started our tank and moved very slowly forward (creeping), I suddenly noticed that the Tiger was moving out of its position and had exposed its belly to us. I immediately put an AP shell into its belly and knocked it off. The second AP shot was fired at its tracks and knocked the right track off. The third shot (HE point detonating) was fired at the turret and destroyed the escaping crew.

Mashlonik went on to knock out three Panzer IVs at a range of 1,200 yards with just one 90-mm round apiece, so he was well pleased with the results of his morning's work. This action took place as a follow-up to the knocking out of a Pershing by a Tiger which was discussed earlier.

M36 Tank Destroyer Although strictly not a tank, but rather a tank destroyer (TD), the U.S. Army's M36 (based on the M10A1 but with a larger turret) also mounted a 90-mm gun that could knock out a Tiger at a reasonable range. On the plus side M36s started to arrive in north-west Europe in September 1944, so were available, for example, during the Battle of the Bulge. However, the TD had an open-topped turret

While the Tigers are well hidden in the wood the track marks remain a dead give-away from the air and will invite a call from the Jabos unless blotted out. (BA 22/2935/19A)

(although later, a folding armored top was fitted on the M36B2) and its armor thickness was only 50 mm, so although it was often used as a tank it was extremely vulnerable. Nevertheless, it was one of the very few Allied AFVs that could knock out a Tiger in 1944.

The Sherman Firefly. The big punch in the troops of British armored regiments was the 17-pounder of the Sherman Firefly, normally issued on a scale of one per troop. It still had to have some good luck to knock out a Tiger in a tank engagement, especially as its rate of fire was slow because of the complex procedure that had to be followed when re-loading. *(Compendium)*

Sherman Firefly The only problem with the Pershing was of course that it did not appear on the battlefield until February 25th, 1945, and then only in small numbers. However, the British forces had a Tiger tamer in service a year earlier, from February 1944, when they managed to mount the British 17-pounder gun on three types of American Sherman: the Firefly IIC (on a Sherman M4A1), the Firefly IVC (on a Sherman M4A3) and the Firefly VC (on a Sherman M4A4). While this did raise the firepower, it did nothing to improve the Sherman's lack of protection—not for nothing had it acquired the nickname "Tommy Cooker." However, the Firefly was capable of knocking out a Tiger, which an ordinary Sherman armed with either its original 75-mm gun, or even the more powerful 76-mm, could not hope to achieve even at close range. A tank commander in one of the British Cromwell-equipped armored regiments once told me that the remainder of the troop would not move forward an inch without their accompanying Firefly. "The main reason for this," he said, "was that we had seen the 17-pounder anti-tank gun in action in Tunisia and were well aware that it could knock out a Tiger front on."

M10 Achilles In the same way as the M36 tank destroyer mounted a gun capable of dealing with the Tiger, so did another TD, namely the British version of the M10/M10A1 Wolverine, which was fitted with the same British 17-pounder as mounted on the Sherman Firefly. It was known as Achilles (IC was the conversion from the M10 and IIC from the M10A1). As the 17-pounder gun tube was smaller in diameter than the American 3-inch gun (normal main armament for the M10 Wolverine) a special casting had to be welded over the gunshield to reduce the size of the hole. An additional counterweight was also added to the end of the barrel just behind the muzzle brake.

IS-2 and IS-3 While the Russian KV-1 and KV-2 heavy tanks were no match for Tiger, their successors in the Josef Stalin series were a different proposition entirely, especially the IS-2 and IS-3, that were both armed with 122-mm guns of comparable hitting power with the 8.8-cm and, in addition were well armored, the glacis plate and armor layout being designed to give maximum ballistic protection. Both entered service in 1944 and, while the IS-3 only saw limited action in the last few months of the war, the IS-2 was in operational service during the first half of 1944 and quickly showed that its firepower and protection were of a

Another Tiger tamer was the Soviet Josef Stalin series of which the IS-3 (known as the "Pike" because of its pointed front glacis) was undoubtedly the best. However, IS-3 did not enter service until late 1944, while IS-2 (1944) and IS-1 (1943), the former known as the "Victory Tank," were both in service in reasonable quantity to have an effect on the battlefields. *(Author's Collection)*

Main armament on Tiger, Pershing, Firefly and IS-3

Tank	Weapon	Length in calibers overall	Length (in)
Tiger I	8.8-cm KwK 36 L/56	56	209
Tiger II	8.8-cm KwK 43 L/71	71	256
Jagdtiger	12.8-cm KwK	43	260
Pershing	90-mm M3	53	202
Firefly	17-pdr Mk IV	55	184
IS-3	122-mm M1943	45	238

Armor Penetration (Ammunition as shown)

Tank	Ammo type	Muzzle velocity (ft per sec)	Penetration (mm) at ranges in yards			
			500	1,000	1,500	2,000
Tiger I	APCBC	2,660	110	101	93	84
	APCR	3,070	126	103	85	70
Tiger II	APCBC	3,340	182	167	153	139
Jagdtiger	APC	2,890	175	150	132	120
	APCBC	3,020	215	202	190	178
Pershing	APCBC	2,650	126	120	114	105
	HVAP	3,350	221	200	177	154
Firefly	APCBC	2,900	125	118	110	98
	APDS	3,950	187	170	153	135
IS-3	APCBC	2,450	140	130	120	110

Note: Penetration is in mm against homogeneous armor plate at 30 degrees.

Source: P. Hordern, *Fire and Movement*, published by U.K. Tank Museum

high order. One "Notes to Panzer Troops" contained an article entitled "Tiger versus Stalin" (repeated in an MI 10 circular to British troops in 1945) which said:

> Stalin tanks can be brewed up, although penetration is by no means easy against the frontal armor at long ranges (another Tiger battalion reports that Stalin tanks can only be penetrated by Tigers frontally under 550 yards) . . . Stalin tanks should, wherever possible, be engaged in flanks or rear and destroyed by concentrated fire . . . Stalin tanks should not be engaged under any circumstances by Tigers in less than troop strength. To use single Tigers is to invite their destruction.

On the other side of the hill the accounts of remarkable engagements in which a handful of Tigers came out on top are legion— here are two. The first is from Italy, where in some areas the countryside was ideal for long-range engagements, especially if the Tigers were in

OPPOSITE: Good close-up of a motorcycle with sidecar. It is a BMW R75 which was a special military design; over 16,500 were produced during the war. It was powered by an HO 2-cylinder 26-bhp engine. This one was photographed during bitter winter weather in March 1944. *(BA 279/946/20)*

good defensive positions. One of these engagements took place on June 22nd, 1944, shortly after Heavy Tank Battalion 504's return to the line near Massa Marittima. A single Tiger platoon of four tanks stopped the *entire* U.S. Fifth Army in its tracks near Parolla, knocking out eleven of the twenty-three Sherman tanks that were leading the American assault. "Like shooting ducks on a pond" was the German verdict on the engagement and the Sherman crews had to agree. The remaining dozen Shermans were abandoned by their crews during the action and were all captured by the Tigers during the counter-attack that followed.

The second engagement has got to be Michael Wittmann versus the entire 4 CLY advance guard of 7th Armoured Division at Villers-Bocage. The Desert Rats had just performed a daring right hook aimed at the small town and the high ground to its north-east. However, little did they known that Wittmann and six of his Tiger Is (of which only three were fully fit) had spent the night just to the north-east of Villers-Bocage. It was difficult to know who were the more surprised, Wittmann and his Tiger crews, who watched amazed from their bivouac area as the British column advanced leisurely toward them, or Lieutenant-Colonel Lord Cranley, CO of 4 CLY, and his mixed force of tanks and motorized infantry (in half-tracks), who clearly had no idea that the enemy were almost within touching distance. When the action began Cranley was up with the advance guard who, after receiving a generous welcome from the citizens of Villers-Bocage, were taking few proper precautions against the possibility of bumping the enemy. The Germans were the first to react, Wittmann leaping on board one of the three fit tanks (his own would not start), exiting the bivouac area, and racing down the road past the surprised enemy column, then engaging the last two AFVs of A Squadron, a Cromwell and a Sherman Firefly, knocking them both out and thus effectively blocking the road back into the town. His other tanks immediately opened fire on the leading British tanks (Cromwells), rapidly knocking them all out. Wittmann himself, continued on into town, shooting up the assorted vehicles as he passed them by, his 8.8-cm and coaxial machine gun making short work of the lightly armored British force. In town his rampage eventually came to an end, when his tank was knocked out by fire from a well-placed 6-pounder anti-tank gun, but Wittmann and his crew managed to bail out unharmed, and made it on foot to the HQ of the Panzer Lehr Division some four miles to the north. The entire battle lasted under one quarter of an hour, but in that time Wittmann's *personal* tally was seven cruiser/medium tanks (including one Firefly), one Sherman OP, nine halftracks, four carriers and two anti-tank guns. The rest of his Tigers dealt with the others, then took the majority of the advance guard prisoner, including Lord Cranley. Wittmann would be awarded his Swords and promoted to captain for this action, which proved to be

The Russian Menace

"The appearance of the new Russian heavy tanks accelerated the attempts that had been in progress in Germany since 1937 to construct a more powerful tank possessing greater combat capabilities. The construction of a heavy tank that could be superior to the new Russian tanks and which could reach the front quickly was the order of the day. The race to build Germany's best and most powerful tank had begun."

From: *Tiger, The History of a Legendary Weapon*, Egon Kleine and Volkmar Kühn

his swansong, as he was killed a few weeks later on August 8th at Gaumesnil, south of Caen, by Sherman Fireflies of the Northamptonshire Yeomanry.

Tiger I Analysis

In his biography of Michael Wittmann, Gary L. Simpson includes a useful short summary of the good and bad points of Tiger I; the most important ones appear in the table overleaf. Some of the failings listed were rectified in Tiger II and there were other improvements made—such as the turret now being large enough to take the improved KwK 43 L/71 gun, giving even better penetrative power. However, the streamlined Porsche turret (fitted to the first fifty produced) had a "shot trap" formed by the curved front of the turret, which then had to be eliminated—the redesigned Henschel turret eliminating this problem by decreasing the frontal area of the turret and gun mantlet. Additionally, frontal armor thickness was increased to 150 mm and the hull was similar in design to Panther, while the suspension now consisted of nine sets of interlaced roadwheels sprung on torsion bars (similar to Panther, but with one more set of roadwheels).

As Tigers were so difficult to penetrate, experienced opponents would seek other ways of disabling them, for example directing concentrated fire on the vision devices to blind the crew, or on the

The major problem with Tiger was its weight, which made it difficult for the heavy tank battalions to use the same routes as other lighter AFVs. This was a problem especially on the Eastern Front in the spring and fall when the ground was usually soft and Tigers would often get bogged down and need recovery. *(BA 1011276/701/14)*

Tiger I—Strengths and Weaknesses

Strengths

- Powerful 8.8-cm main gun easily stripped for maintenance.
- Well-constructed with heavy armor to give good protection.
- Stable gun platform
- Ammunition stowage quantity (92 rounds carried—but 20 fewer in Tiger II)
- Ammunition readily accessible
- Electrical firing gear, with safety interlocks
- Flush turret floor
- Binocular telescope for gunner
- Mounting for periscope binoculars (for commander) in cupola, plus hand traverse, with an override
- Plenty of space for the loader to deal with the long, heavy round
- Spring-loaded turret hatches
- Three-position commander's seat, with backrest
- Electrically fired smoke generator dischargers

Weaknesses

- Gun and turret out of balance
- Obscuration due to smoke from flashless propellant
- Bad ventilation from gun fumes
- Loader has no intercom
- Commander and gunner have cramped positions
- Awkward powered-traverse control
- Ammunition bins unarmored
- Gun deflector bag (for spent cartridge cases) too small
- Difficult to reload coaxial MG
- Gunner must exit via commander's cupola

OPPOSITE: Winter in Russia and, like their tanks, the crews wore white—namely, two-piece snowsuits (*Schneeanzüge*). The special rations being handed out were possibly to celebrate New Year 1944. (BA 278/874/7)

running gear, or against all visible parts of the formidable 8.8-cm gun.

It is also clear from the after-action reports that Tiger was, at times, a victim of its own success and, undoubtedly, also of the "spin" put on its comparative invulnerability by German propaganda. For example, one Tiger battalion CO wrote:

> The extensive propaganda in the newspapers touts the Tiger as being invulnerable and pure life insurance, so the higher command as well as the simple infantry soldier believe they can continuously accomplish everything with this fortress.

How can we best summarise the true situation? Perhaps the most succinct statement was one written in a captured German report, circulated by 21st Army Group to the Allied forces in France in June 1944, which read as follows:

When Tigers first appeared on the battlefield, they were in every respect proof against enemy weapons. They quickly won for themselves the title of "unbeatable" and "undamageable." But in the meantime, the enemy has not been asleep. Anti-tank guns, tanks, and mines have been developed which can hit a Tiger hard and even knock it out. Now the Tiger, for a long time regarded as a "life insurance policy," is relegated to the ranks of simply a "heavy tank" … No longer can the Tiger prance around oblivious of the laws of tank tactics. It must obey these laws, just as every other tank must. So remember you men who fight in Tiger tanks—DON'T demand the impossible from your Tiger and DO just what your commanding officer orders. He knows the limitations of his vehicles and guns, and knows the best use to which they should be put . . .

REFERENCE

Current Locations—Tiger I

There are currently just five known Tiger Is in existence outside Russia.

Turret No. 131 was abandoned by its crew (from s.Pz-Abt 504) in Tunisia after an action involving Churchill tanks of 48th RTR. This tank was later brought back to the U.K. and sent to the School of Tank Technology at Chertsey, where it was closely examined and a detailed report written. Subsequently it was one of the nucleus of WWII vehicles that joined the U.K. Tank Museum, Bovington, Dorset, postwar. After it had been many years on static display, it was decided to put the vehicle back into full running order once the necessary finance had been obtained. This was eventually achieved in the mid-nineties and, after a

Tiger I (Turret No 131) captured in Tunisia in April 1943, is seen here during the 2006 "Tankfest," held at the U.K. Tank Museum, Bovington, Dorset. *(Tank Museum 6399/D3)*

decade of hard work, Turret No. 131 took part in the Tank Museum's "Tankfest" in September 2006 for the very first time and proved to be a star attraction.

Turret No. 712, belonging to s.Pz-Abt 501, was also captured in Tunisia, and was earmarked for the U.S.A. It was taken to the Aberdeen Proving Ground, Maryland, after the war had ended, for examination by U.S. Army Ordnance personnel. It later joined the "outside collection" at APG and remained there for many years, out in all weathers, until the 1980s, when a deal was struck with the Autotechnik Museum at Sinsheim near Heidelberg for the Tiger I, plus two other AFVs, to be given to Sinsheim, who were hoping to put it back into running order, but sadly were unable to make any progress. Enter Kevin Wheatcroft, owner of the Wheatcroft Collection of historic vehicles, weapons, and AFVs from World War II, located in Leicestershire, England. Mr Wheatcroft is an avowed Tiger enthusiast, who has been collecting Tiger parts for many years—his aim being, one day, to build a Tiger II. As anyone who has delved into the AFV restoration business knows, it is difficult, slow, and very expensive, especially when one is dealing with 60-odd years old, 60–70 ton vehicles, that have been standing out in the open most of those years, prey to the weather and to petty pilfering from souvenir hunters. Mr Wheatcroft was asked to safeguard all three AFVs until APG/Sinsheim had raised the money to restore them. Sadly that is how the situation remains today. The restoration has halted awaiting further developments.

A third Tiger I resides at the French Tank Museum, Saumur.

The fourth is still in a roadside location in Normandy at Vimoutiers, north-east of Argentan.

A fifth is at present only a collection of parts from which Mr Wheatcroft aims to build another Tiger I.

It is thought that there are others in Russian collections and it is possible that more Tigers will be recovered from the lakes and forests in Poland, the Baltic States, and Russia, but of course that is pure speculation.

Current Locations—Tiger II

At least seven or eight Tiger IIs are still in existence.

There are two Tiger IIs in the U.K., one (Porsche turret) that has long been in the WWII hall at the Tank Museum, where it was recently joined (early 2006) by a Henschel-turreted version that had resided at the Royal Military College of Science, Shrivenham, since the end of the war. Both are non-runners.

A Henschel-turreted version is on display at the Panzer Museum, Münster, Germany. It is in reasonable condition but not in working order.

Many books with information about Tiger are available; it is probably the single most popular tank of World War II. (*J. Forty*)

The Tiger II (Henschel turret) going through its paces at the French Tank Museum's annual display at Saumur. *(Tank Museum 4819/G1)*

There is another Tiger II (Henschel turret) in the French Tank Museum, Saumur, which has been in full working order and participated in the museum's displays.

The Russians also have a Tiger II (Henschel turret) in their Tank Museum at Kubinka, some twenty-five miles from Moscow.

A sixth Tiger II (Henschel turret) is in a roadside location at La Gleize, Belgium.

The seventh is in the Swiss Army base at Thun—basically complete but a non-runner with some external damage including the end of the gun barrel missing (shot off in combat).

The eighth is in Kevin Wheatcroft's collection, some seventy-five percent complete and made up of items collected from three tanks. The wheels, tracks, main armament, engine, radiators, internal parts, and hull all exist. Currently he has some seventy-five percent of the turret missing together with the transmission and turret ring.

Replicas From time to time replicas are made for use in war films such as *Kelly's Heroes* (1970). However, the latest and possibly the most realistic, were two Tiger Is (based on two Soviet T-34s) made for use in the movie *Saving Private Ryan*.

Variants

Jagdtiger Only two Jagdtigers are known to exist. One is in the U.K. Tank Museum and the other at the Aberdeen Proving Ground.

The Tiger II (Porsche turret) in the World War II display at the U.K. Tank Museum. *(Tank Museum 4892/E6)*

Sturmmörser Tiger Just one is known to exist. For some years it was also in the APG collection, after an initial detailed evaluation in the U.K. However, a few years ago it was returned to Germany and is now part of the Technical Defense Studies Collection at Koblenz. The gun tube belonging to this AFV is currently with the U.K. Tank Museum.

Front page of the Achtung Panzer! site.

Internet Sites

Over 73,000 sites seem to have Tiger information, covering a bewildering array of interests including highly detailed histories with extensive photo collections as well as sites specifically for wargamers, modellers, computer gamers, etc.

www.achtungpanzer.com An interesting site with very detailed information on German armor; great pictures of preserved machines.

www.feldgrau.com This site is probably the most comprehensive

PzKpfw VI Tiger I tactical number B01 of the 10th company of the III Abteilung of the "Großdeutschland" Division passing in front of some divisional vehicles.

The home page at fprado.com, naturally featuring a fine illustration of a Tiger I.

resource currently available on the web which deals with all the German armed forces before and during WWII.

www.alanhamby.com/tiger.html Comprehensive site, Tiger information center, with extensive production and unit histories, and many photos.

www.worldwar2aces.com/tiger-tank/tiger-tank.htm Interesting photo gallery.

www.fprado.com/armorsite/tigers.htm The life and times of Germany's Tiger tank battalions.

Critical Bibliography

For an excellent selection of books about Tiger and its wartime history, I strongly recommend Barbarossa Books of Tiptree Essex (<sales@barbarossabooks.co.uk>; tel: +44 (0)1621 810810). For out-of-print titles amazon.com is the best source.

Chamberlain, Peter, and Hilary L. Doyle: *Encyclopedia of German Tanks of World War II*, Arms and Armour Press, 1978. Probably the best enyclopedia of the subject available.

Fellgiebel, Major (retd.) Walther-Peer (translated by C. F. Colton and Duncan Rogers): *Elite of the Third Reich*, Helion, 2003. Originally published in German in 2000 by Podzun-Pallas Verlag, this is a remarkable work of reference that lists all the recipients of the Knight's Cross—over 7,000 of them! Also included are details of recipients of higher classes of the decoration. Major Fellgiebel is the Chairman of the Awards Committee of the Confraternity of Recipients of the Knight's Cross, so its accuracy is second to none and I have used it above all other references to construct my roll-call in the Personalities section above.

Fletcher, David, ed.: *Tiger!—The Tiger Tank: A British View*, HMSO, 1986. A factual record of the various British investigations into the Tiger tank. It is divided into four parts: an introduction which endeavors to uncover some of the mystique surrounding Tiger; a selection of items showing the Allied reaction to the new tank, from the first notification of its existence by Military Intelligence up to the arrival of a fully working Tiger in the U.K.; a copy of the School of Tank Technology and Military College of Science report which detailed the extensive examination of Tiger that was issued postwar; finally a section of the book deals with those aspects of Tiger which came to light postwar. All in all it is an excellent book, crammed with facts and figures, photographs and line drawings, information, and comment. I am very surprised that it has never been reprinted.

Front page of the alanhanby.com website, featuring one of the many photos, diagrams, and artworks viewable in this resource.

Forty, George: *German Tanks of World War Two*, Blandford Press, 1988. A cheap and cheerful history of the German tanks that fought in WWII. It was translated into German in 1998 by Weltbild Verlag of Augsburg, so there can't have been too many mistakes!

Gudgin, Major Peter: *The Tiger Tanks*, Arms and Armour Press, 1991. An excellent study of Tiger, covering its background history, then chapters on the Porsche Tiger, Tiger I, Tiger II, and Jagdtiger, followed by their history in combat. Major Gudgin fought against Tigers in Tunisia and then had a great deal to do with examining Tiger 131, so he is the ideal author of this study—that he managed to cram it all in and still keep his book a fascinating read shows considerable skill. The ideal first book for anyone wanting to start looking into the story of this remarkable family of tanks. Second-hand copies are still available via amazon.com.

Jentz, Thomas L.: *Panzer Truppen 1—1933–1942*; *Panzer Truppen 2—1943–1945*; *Tigers at the Front*; Schiffer Military History, 1996, 1996, 2001. These are but three of the numerous books on the Tiger family that Tom Jentz has published for Schiffer Military History. They are all of the same high standard, as one would expect from Jentz and Schiffer, whose work is much admired on both sides of the Atlantic

Kleine, Egon, and Volkmar Kühn: *Tiger, The History of a Legendary Weapon 1942–45*, J. J. Fedorowicz Publishing, 1989. Originally published in German by Motorbuch Verlag of Stuttgart, this is crammed with information, first-hand accounts, photographs and maps, etc., giving a vivid, if slightly difficult to follow, account of everything about the Tiger and its battles from the very beginning. Like Schiffer in the U.S.A, J. J. Fedorowicz of Canada has a worldwide reputation for the excellence of its military literature and this book is no exception.

Nafziger, George F.: *The German Order of Battle—Panzers and Artillery in WWII*, Greenhill Books, 1999. A comprehensive study of German WWII organizations by a world-renowned historian, specialising in studies of organizational tables of WWII and the Napoleonic period. He naturally includes the heavy tank battalions (in a separate section).

Restayn, Jean: *Tiger I on the Eastern Front* and *Tiger I on the Western Front*, Histoires et Collections, 1999, 2001. As one might expect from this renowned military author, both these books are packed with information, an excellent selection of photographs, and, best of all, the author's colored line drawings which are magnificent! Having had his books for a number of years I did not think they could be beaten; however, that was before I obtained Schneider and Wilbeck (*see below*).

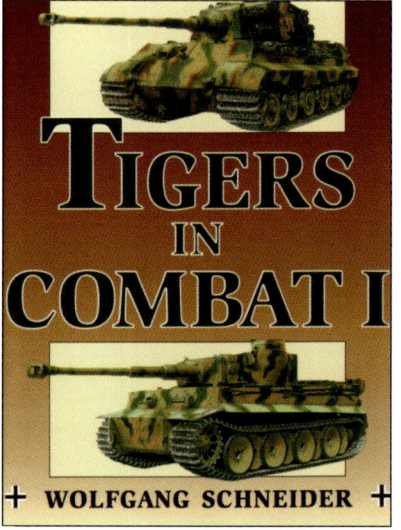

The first volume of Wolfgang Schnieder's highly recommended study of the Tiger. *(J. Forty)*

Schneider, Wolfgang: *Tigers in Combat*, Vols 1 and 2, J. J. Fedorowicz Publishing (hardback) 1998 and 2000, Stackpole Books (softback) 2004 and 2005. Colonel Schneider's two volumes are a mammoth detailed study of the German wartime heavy tank battalions, covering their history from inception to war's end. With a total of over 650 large pages, crammed with facts, figures, tables, drawings, photographs (over 500), maps, and Jean Restayn's incomparable colored drawings, Schneider has produced a feast for all Tiger enthusiasts!

Simpson, Gary L.: *The Life Story of Panzer Commander Michael Wittmann*, Schiffer Military History, 1994. An interesting and detailed biography of one of the most famous tank aces of WWII. It includes some rarely seen photographs of Wittmann.

Wilbeck, Major Christopher W.: *Sledgehammers—Strengths and Flaws of Tiger Tank Battalions in World War II*, The Aberjona Press, 2004. Major Wilbeck has done an excellent, meticulous job, as one would expect from a professional—he was a member of the U.S. 1st Cavalry Division and took part in both the Desert Shield and Desert Storm operations. His book is a well-written, thoughtful study of the subject. I bow to the excellence of his work! Highly recommended.

There are many more books about the Tiger; space does not permit me to mention more than just a handful. Some of the best are Polish/English bilingual publications which contain detailed 1:35 scale plans as well as photographs and plenty of text (in English and Polish). Examples are:

> Trojca W.: Trojca Series No. 12, *Königstiger Vol 1* and No. 14, *Königstiger Vol 2.*
> Melleman T.: Tank Power Series No. 16, Vol IV, *Sturmtiger.*

While it is possible to make choices off the net it is still very worthwhile contacting a specialist bookseller like Barbarossa Books for advice before ordering.

Multimedia

Cassell Publishing (U.K.) and the Tamiya model company have produced an interactive CD-Rom *PzKpfw VI Tiger Tank* which features rare archive footage, contemporary film footage, and many still photographs, including internal and external 360-degree panoramic images of the inside and outside of the Tiger heavy tank, plus detailed color drawings and plans, markings and camouflage guides, technical data files, development and in-service histories, and much more—as they say on the sleeve: "everything but the smell!"

Saving the Tiger The U.K. Tank Museum has produced a DVD about the capture of Tiger 131 from the Tunisian battlefields, and its subsequent restoration to full working order. Available from <www.tankmuseum.co.uk>.

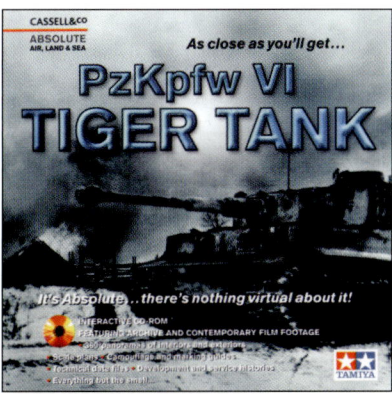

The Tiger interactive CD-Rom produced by Cassell and Tamiya is a must for all Tiger enthusiasts. *(J. Forty)*

The Tank Museum's DVD re-tells the wartime history and the recent restoration of Tiger 131. *(J. Forty)*

INDEX

INDEX